Effective group work with young people

Effective group work with young people

Jane Westergaard

 McGraw Hill

Open University Press

Open University Press
McGraw-Hill Education
McGraw-Hill House
Shoppenhangers Road
Maidenhead
Berkshire
England
SL6 2QL

email: enquiries@openup.co.uk
world wide web: www.openup.co.uk

and Two Penn Plaza, New York, NY 10121–2289, USA

First published 2009

A catalogue record of this book is available from the British Library

ISBN-13: 978 0 335 23418 9 (pb)   978 0 335 23417 2 (hb)
ISBN-10: 0 335 23418 6 (pb)   0 335 23417 8 (hb)

Library of Congress Cataloging-in-Publication Data
CIP data applied for

Typeset by RefineCatch Limited, Bungay, Suffolk
Printed in the UK by Bell and Bain Ltd, Glasgow

Mixed Sources
Product group from well-managed
forests and other controlled sources
www.fsc.org Cert no. TT-COC-002769
© 1996 Forest Stewardship Council

The McGraw·Hill Companies

Contents

Acknowledgements

I am indebted to Ruth Higgins, Dr Hazel Reid and Tamsin Stubbs for their help, support and expertise in writing this book. Many thanks also to Mike Westergaard for providing the illustrations.

Preface

Why do we need another book about group work?

Good question. There are various resources that focus on delivering group work to young people in a range of contexts, most notably in relation to informal education, counselling and therapy. There is also a range of literature that concentrates on developing task-oriented and project-driven groups. This book though is different. It relates to another type of group work: one which is concerned with young people's *personal learning and development* (PLD), delivered in an educational context by a professional who is not a qualified teacher. Simply put, PLD group work pays attention to the issues and needs that affect young people's lives. Previously, these sessions may have been termed 'life skills', but this title does not give sufficient weight to the complexity of issues and topics discussed; from confidence building and anger management to sexual health and drugs awareness. The purpose of PLD group work then is to encourage young people to explore and share their thoughts, feelings and experiences in order to increase self-awareness and work towards positive change in their lives. Personal learning and development takes place when youth support workers plan and prepare group sessions that are largely experiential and interactive, providing opportunities for young people to learn from each other in a structured way.

So, this book aims to provide a helpful, practical resource for those who are involved in delivering PLD sessions. It offers guidance on planning and preparation, suggestions for structuring group work, ideas for group activities, advice on developing facilitation skills and strategies for managing challenging behaviour. In addition, it provides a sound theoretical underpinning by introducing key concepts such as learning theory and group dynamics. In short, this book is a one-stop guide to planning and delivering PLD group work.

Who is the book for?

Another good question! The book has been written with a range of practitioners in mind. As suggested previously, it is aimed primarily at those professionals who support young people (or are training to do so) in an established educational context, but who are not trained teachers. The range of roles includes teaching assistants, learning mentors, personal advisers, careers advisers, classroom assistants, youth workers, health workers and others who are working with young people. Often these 'youth support workers' (this generic term is used throughout the book) have had little experience or training in group work. However, they may find themselves occasionally in situations where they are asked to undertake work with groups of young people, or, alternatively, group work may be a central aspect of their role. In either case, those who have found themselves faced with delivering group work to young people for the first time will know that it can be a daunting experience. This book should go some way to reducing those feelings of anxiety as it offers a step-by-step guide to facilitating PLD sessions with both small and class-sized groups. The book also provides a useful resource for teachers, trainers and anyone else concerned with the development of young people's self-awareness, personal and life skills (e.g. through citizenship, personal, social and health education or a life skills programme).

How should the book be used?

The book has been structured to provide guidance and support through the process of planning, preparing, delivering and evaluating group sessions; although each chapter can be accessed in a 'stand-alone' capacity if specific guidance is needed in relation to a particular aspect of group work.

Chapter 1 begins by setting out the range of roles that constitute 'youth support'. Using a case study approach, it provides examples of the types of group session facilitated by youth support workers. It goes on to establish the meaning of personal learning and development group work by comparing PLD sessions with teaching, informal education and therapeutic groups.

In Chapter 2, the concept of personal learning and development is explored in more depth, with particular emphasis placed on learning: what learning means, how it happens and how youth support workers can facilitate it effectively. Again, case study examples are used to illustrate the theory and concepts discussed and to provide an opportunity for readers to reflect on the application of learning theory to their practice.

Chapters 3–6 are concerned with the chronology of the planning process. These chapters suggest a framework for the preparation of sessions: assessing the needs of young people and identifying a relevant topic, setting a session aim and objectives, selecting appropriate activities, structuring the session and preparing a detailed session plan. Using five case studies (Lloyd the learning mentor, Ashraf the personal adviser, Crystal the careers adviser, Jatinder the teenage pregnancy adviser and Sam the youth worker) to illustrate and 'follow through' the planning process, readers will have the opportunity to reflect on their own approaches to preparing for group sessions.

Chapter 7 explores key facilitation skills and techniques that youth support workers should develop in order to undertake PLD group work effectively. It 'names' the skills and suggests how and when they should be used in group sessions with young people.

Chapter 8 introduces the concept of group dynamics. It identifies theories and analytical frameworks that aid understanding about why being part of a group might have an impact on how young people may present themselves. Again, case studies are used to illustrate the ways in which the dynamic of the group could have an impact on the session.

Chapter 9 is concerned with managing challenging behaviour. Of course, if sessions are carefully planned, then the risk of encountering disruptive or challenging behaviour should be minimized. However, youth support workers are likely, at some point in their careers, to experience behaviour that requires careful handling. This chapter provides some useful strategies to consider, using case studies in order to bring the examples to life. Finally, Chapter 10 reflects on the importance of evaluating PLD group work and provides examples of the kinds of evaluation tool that might be used.

Each chapter features suggested activities and questions to stimulate thought and aid reflection. The reader is asked to think about and apply their learning to their own practice in group work. Those involved in educating youth support workers may also find the activities useful as a starting point for discussion. Where appropriate, suggestions have been made for further reading.

And finally . . .

Above all else, this book is aimed at being a practical and accessible resource. It should provide support to any practitioner who at some point in their professional life undertakes group work, the purpose of which is to enable young people to work towards making positive change in their lives.

1

The role of youth support workers with groups of young people

Learning Objectives

· Identify the role of the youth support worker
· Describe the role of the youth support worker in relation to facilitating group sessions
· Define personal learning and development (PLD) group work
· Identify the key features of PLD group sessions
· Describe the differences between PLD group sessions and other forms of group activity

Introduction

The changing education landscape in recent years has placed an emphasis on employing a range of individuals whose role is to provide 'support' to students. The focus in teaching and learning has been informed by an argument for greater emphasis on the *individual* and supporting them in meeting their needs. What this support consists of and who delivers it is not always easy to unravel. There is an ever-increasing list of job titles that describe specific functions for those who work closely with young people in schools and colleges, but who are not themselves teachers. These 'para-professionals' make up a significant proportion of the work force in secondary schools and further education colleges, and in the UK these roles include teaching assistants, classroom assistants and learning mentors. In the USA, Europe and Scandinavia alternative job titles describe similar roles: tutors, learning support staff or student advisers for example. There will be others for whom the support of young people in education is central to their work; however, they are not based permanently in educational institutions, but are regular visitors to them. These 'visiting' youth support professionals are likely to include careers' advisers, personal advisers, school counsellors, and youth, community and health workers. It would be foolish to argue that this wealth of support for young people is not welcome – it is. But it would also be true to say that for many working in education, including teachers and managers, the plethora of roles can lead to confusion.

Much of the support provided by those in the roles outlined above is likely to be one to one, whereby helping relationships are established between a young person and an identified worker. Through these relationships, the individual needs of the young person are recognized and strategies for development and change are discussed and implemented. However, increasingly youth support workers are finding themselves in situations where they are working with groups of young people, not just individuals, in order to offer support. Initially, providing support in a group context may feel daunting, as many youth support workers will not have had extensive training in how to prepare, plan and deliver group learning. However, it is important to recognize the benefits of offering support to young people through group work as well as in one-to-one relationships. Group work provides youth support workers with the opportunity to access and utilize possibly the greatest 'support' resource they will have at their disposal – the young people themselves.

This chapter begins by focusing on the range of youth support roles currently in evidence in schools and colleges and it 'unpicks' the key tasks undertaken by these youth support workers. Once the range of youth support work roles has been examined, the chapter establishes the *key features* of group work that takes place in educational environments (e.g. school, college), but is *not* delivered by teachers or those with extensive training in learning and teaching methods. The distinction between 'supporting' group work, which focuses on the group members' 'personal learning and development', and other activities, which involve young people working together in a group in educational settings, will be made clear. The chapter compares PLD group work delivered by youth support workers with three other forms of group activity:

- teaching;
- informal education;
- therapeutic groups.

By undertaking a comparison of teaching, informal education and therapeutic group work, the distinctive features of PLD group work will be made clear. But first, who are these youth support workers and what do they do?

The youth support worker role

A visit to any secondary school or further education college in the UK (and in many other countries in Europe and throughout the world) will introduce the visitor to a range of professionals who are working together to support students and to ensure that young people are encouraged and enabled to achieve their full potential. The case studies that follow will help to provide some clarity about the range of youth support roles in education (note: all case study examples used throughout the book are drawn from experience, but do not represent real people or institutions).

Kelly – the teaching assistant in Manor Way School

Kelly works with designated students who have been identified as needing additional support in the classroom. Kelly's role is to accompany these students to lessons and to plan with each individual subject teacher how she can support these young people in the classroom. This support may involve assisting with literacy and numeracy, or it may require Kelly to offer help in dealing with emotional or behavioural problems. Sometimes, the students who Kelly supports are disruptive in class. On a number of occasions Kelly has been asked to work with small groups of young people away from the classroom to assist them to develop their personal skills.

Lloyd – the learning mentor in Manor Way School

Lloyd, like Kelly, works with pupils who have been assigned to him for additional support. The young people Lloyd works with have poor attendance records and are at risk of exclusion. Lloyd supports these young people on a one-to-one basis, inside the classroom and outside it. He also works with groups of young people who have been identified as needing help with particular issues such as anger management or family breakdown.

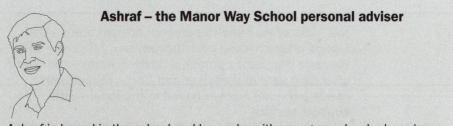

Ashraf – the Manor Way School personal adviser

Ashraf is based in the school and he works with young people who have been referred to him because they are experiencing barriers to progression. These barriers might include disruptive behaviour, lack of confidence or other issues including poor housing, risk of exclusion or social problems like bullying. Ashraf works on a one-to-one basis with young people, but he also runs group sessions when shared issues or problems emerge with students in the school.

Sam – the youth worker employed by the local youth service

Sam is not based permanently in the school. But he visits every evening to work as part of an extended schools project where students (and their families) are invited to use the facilities of the school to encourage their development outside school hours. Sam works with groups of young people who have been identified as needing support with personal and social issues. He runs group sessions on confidence building, assertiveness, drug and alcohol awareness and team building.

Crystal – the careers adviser based in the local careers centre

Like Sam, Crystal is not based in the school, but visits regularly to talk to individual students about their options and progression during and after school. Crystal mainly works on a one-to-one basis with young people, but she also delivers group sessions on topics like job applications, CV writing and interview skills.

Joe – the sexual health personal adviser, Julie – the looked after children personal adviser, Jatinder – the teenage pregnancy personal adviser, Karin – the youth offending personal adviser and Carl – the intensive needs personal adviser based in the local youth support service

Joe, Julie, Jatinder, Karin and Carl are not based in the school, but are frequent visitors to it. Young people are referred to them as needs are identified by teachers in the school. They work with 'targeted' young people on a one-to-one basis, but they also work with groups when appropriate. Jatinder, for example, is delivering a 'cyber baby' course (where young people prepare to look after a 'baby', programmed to cry and demand attention) to a group of 16-year-old girls.

Pat – pupil referral unit worker

Pat works in the Pupil Referral Unit that is attached to Manor Way School with young people who have been excluded. These young people have not responded positively to the school environment or are school-phobic. Like many of the other youth support roles, Pat offers one-to-one help and he also undertakes group work that focuses on the personal learning and development needs of pupils in the unit.

This is a brief and by no means comprehensive glimpse of the range of para-professionals working in one school and its associated services. All the roles identified involve building one-to-one relationships with young people, and this element of youth support work is dealt with extensively on training courses and through the literature (de Shazer, 1994; Egan, 2002; Nelson-Jones, 2005; Reid and Fielding, 2007). However, what has become clear is that youth support work is not focused solely on one-to-one work with young people. In all the case studies outlined above, group sessions form an aspect of the work. So, what kind of group work do youth support workers deliver and how is it different from other forms of group activity?

What is a group?

The concept of 'a group' is familiar to us all. We are each likely to be involved in groups as part of our everyday lives. For example, we are almost certainly members of a family group, a friendship group, a group of colleagues and other social groups. In addition, we are likely to have played an active part in an educational group (i.e. school) from the age of 5 to 16 and we may, at points in our lives, have accessed other groups: support groups, protest groups, political groups, religious groups, sport groups and special interest groups. Each group would have performed a specific function at a particular time, fulfilling a range of requirements from our very basic human needs (food, warmth, shelter) to more complex emotional and psychological needs (belonging, being loved, being understood, developing knowledge, learning a skill). 'Group work' therefore can mean different things at different times.

However, the purpose of this book is to consider ways in which practitioners can work with a specific kind of group. The definition of this group is: *a group made up of* **individuals** *with* **shared needs** *who will benefit from the opportunity to work with, and learn from others in order to develop skills, knowledge and attitudes.*

What kind of group work takes place in education?

In addition to PLD sessions, there are three recognized forms of structured group work in education in which young people may be engaged. These three group activities are different from the PLD sessions facilitated by youth support workers in significant ways. As stated earlier, the three activities are:

- teaching;
- informal education;
- therapeutic groups.

By examining each of these in some detail and comparing them with PLD sessions, it is possible to distinguish what makes PLD group work delivered by youth support workers different.

Teaching

Teaching has seen a significant shift both in terms of philosophy and delivery in the last 50 years. Gone is the focus on 'chalk and talk', underpinned by an emphasis on the transfer of knowledge from 'expert' to beginner. This has been replaced by the concept of the student as 'learner' (Brandes and Ginnis, 1996), taking an active part in students' learning and gaining knowledge, skills and attitudes by engaging with a range of activities in the classroom. However, in spite of this philosophical shift towards students as engaged participants in their own learning, the focus of teaching tends to remain curriculum-driven and therefore largely abstract. Simply put, this means that the subject matter being taught will, generally, be focused on a preset curriculum. This curriculum is likely to be driven by the need to develop understanding and skills in relation to a specific subject. The level of this understanding will be 'tested' at regular intervals, culminating in a nationally recognized qualification that demonstrates the acquisition of knowledge and competence in a particular field of study.

As part of a nationally set curriculum, most students are required to study specific subjects in schools. These are likely to include English, maths, and science – all subjects which, it could be argued, will be of value in later life, but none of these sets out specifically to address the personal and developmental needs of the individual learner. For example, learning about the 'theory of relativity' does not necessarily meet the individual personal development needs of a 15-year-old, whereas learning about how to 'manage my time effectively' does.

It is the role of teachers to ensure that they plan their lessons based on the requirements of the curriculum, and for many there may be little flexibility in the way in which this is delivered in the classroom. Teachers will be experts in their own academic, creative or technical subject matter and they will strive to make their teaching interesting; to engage and inspire the learner and to encourage success in the subject.

Although teachers will have an understanding of the ways in which young people learn, their primary concern is to deliver knowledge about *something* (i.e. their chosen subject). Those involved in delivering PLD group sessions are more interested in helping young people to acquire knowledge about *someone* (i.e. themselves) rather than a 'subject'. The case study below provides an example of what teaching involves.

Bob – the history teacher in Manor Way School

As a subject teacher, Bob is responsible for ensuring that his teaching adheres to a nationally established curriculum, where he has little choice in selecting the subject matter or topic, but some flexibility in choosing appropriate learning methods. To a large extent, the purpose of Bob's role is to ensure that pupils have knowledge of a specific subject area and will gain a qualification in it. This may encourage pupils to develop an interest in the subject; it may inform future choices they make concerning career, but it is unlikely to have a direct impact on their lives in terms of addressing their personal needs.

There have been recent developments in the UK in relation to the introduction of a social curriculum that includes personal, health and social education (PHSE) and citizenship lessons (Department for Education and Skill, 2003). This goes some way to raising awareness of issues that may impact on young people as they make transitions into adulthood. This aspect of the curriculum bears close resemblance to PLD group work in that it aims to assist young people to understand their world and to consider how they can play an active and useful part in society. It is likely that students will be involved in discussions and will undertake activities to broaden their knowledge and understanding, just as they will in PLD group sessions. Although for the most part, the PHSE curriculum is delivered by teachers, youth support workers are often involved, as their expertise in areas related to personal learning and development is recognized and welcomed.

Informal education

The subject of informal education has been written about extensively in recent years (Jeffs, 2004; Davies, 2005) and many youth workers will have undertaken training in informal education. It is not possible or desirable, within the remit of this book, to explore in depth the theory and concepts underpinning informal education – indeed, that is not the purpose of this book. However, it is important that the distinction between informal education and PLD group work in education settings is made clear.

Adams provides a useful definition of informal education:

Groups are made up of individuals who are defined a 'group' because of a common task. The aim of the group is to achieve the chosen task, such as build a carnival float, organise a party, canoe a river or just have fun together. Facilitating achieving the task is not the only area on which the worker needs to focus – equally important is the individual in the group and the group itself. All three aspects need maintaining by the worker, rather like juggling three balls in the air. If too much attention is paid to one, another may fail.

(Adams, 1993: 311)

What is evident here is that learning takes place by engaging with, and setting out to achieve, a specific task. It is, for example, by building a carnival float or organizing a party that participants begin to work together, to learn more about themselves and to understand how they work with, and fit into, the structure of the group. Similarly, in PLD group sessions, participants are encouraged to address their issues and needs by developing greater self-awareness through working alongside others. However, in PLD sessions this 'learning about self' is achieved in a variety of ways by undertaking a range of activities. These activities would not necessarily focus on one overarching project as described by Adams. In fact, the focus of PLD group work is on the needs of each individual in the group, and activities are planned to enable group members to achieve their own personal outcomes. Thus, the individual group members themselves and not the 'project' or 'task' form the focus of the sessions.

Clearly then there are similarities between informal education and PLD group work. For example, the methods of educating are likely to draw on experiential learning techniques (Kolb, 1984), and the success of the sessions will depend on the relationship between the facilitator/educator and the group. But there are differences too. The PLD session, unlike informal education, is likely to take place in a formal setting and will have preset, specific aims and objectives. These aims and objectives are unlikely to link to a piece of project work (i.e. building a carnival float), but will focus on the individual needs of the group members (i.e. developing anger management techniques). Furthermore, PLD sessions are likely to be bound by time (within a school day) and are less likely to be attended on a voluntary basis.

The case study outlined below provides an example of a piece of informal education group work.

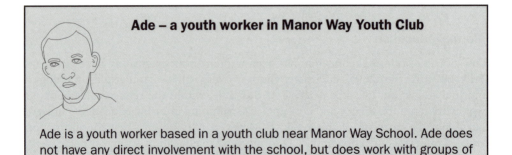

Ade – a youth worker in Manor Way Youth Club

Ade is a youth worker based in a youth club near Manor Way School. Ade does not have any direct involvement with the school, but does work with groups of young people who attend the school. In particular, Ade works with young men who come to the club. He takes groups of young people on residential trips and involves them in project work. The group he is working with currently are helping to develop a plot of scrubland at the back of the youth club into an area where they can play ball games.

Therapeutic group work

Teaching and informal education are examples of two types of group activity that are likely to take place in educational settings. The third, therapeutic group work, delivered by a counsellor, has a different emphasis again. Geldard and Geldard explain:

> Generally, the purpose of therapy groups is to attempt to alleviate specific symptoms or problems (e.g. depression or anxiety). Their focus is either on identifying and treating emotional and/or psychological difficulties seriously interfering with the child's functioning and/or addressing developmental and social problems. Therapy groups are remedial, help to promote personal adjustment and are reconstructive.
>
> (Geldard and Geldard, 2001: 17)

At certain times in the lives of many young people, emotional, psychological and behavioural issues can become hard to manage and seemingly impossible to resolve, resulting in detrimental and sometimes harmful effects. It is during puberty and adolescence that significant physiological and emotional changes are taking place. Many young people are able to 'manage' these changes in a positive way, with the support of family, carers, friends, teachers and others, but some young people struggle to make sense of, and deal with, the new pressures that becoming an adult brings.

It is when barriers to the emotional and psychological development of the young person are identified, and their behaviour is a cause for concern, that it may be helpful to consider counselling or therapy as a means of enabling young people to understand and manage their life better. So, how is counselling or therapy in a group context similar to PLD group sessions, and, importantly, what are the distinctions between the two?

First, both counselling and PLD group work focus on the needs of young people. Both counsellor and facilitator will have an understanding of the issues affecting the group with whom they are working. However, in a counselling setting, it is likely that the issues or 'topic' that forms the focus of the session will require in-depth emotional and psychological exploration and the counsellor will be skilled in enabling this to happen. In PLD sessions, a specific topic or focus for discussion is also identified that meets the individual development needs of the group. However, the PLD topic is less likely to require group members to explore their emotions and psyche in such depth. For example, a school counsellor may work with a group of students who have eating disorders. The counsellor will help the group to explore their feelings, consider causes and work with the emotional trauma present. By contrast, a youth support worker may undertake a PLD session on 'keeping healthy' for a group who have been identified as being 'at risk' of not eating healthily. This session will encourage group members to reflect on their eating habits, to understand more about what healthy eating is and to consider what they need to do in order to eat healthily.

Second, both therapeutic group work and PLD sessions are planned. Group members in both cases will know where the session is being held, how long it will last, why they are there and who will be leading it. However, in the case of counselling sessions, although a broad topic is identified, the agenda for the session is set by the group themselves and the content of the discussion and the issues that are raised are not usually directed by the counsellor. Generally, there are few planned activities within these sessions. Group members are engaged in talking about feelings and the counsellor will use therapeutic techniques to encourage positive change. By contrast, PLD sessions will have been prepared in detail by the facilitator prior to the group meeting. This means that the facilitator will have a session plan that will identify aims and objectives, they will have considered activities to use and they will have identified timings for these activities. Although this plan is negotiated and agreed with the group at the outset, and can be amended if necessary, the PLD session will follow a clear structure.

The third similarity between the two activities is that the aim of each is to work towards positive outcomes. The purpose of both therapeutic groups and PLD sessions is, in part, to enable participants to make some kind of change or development in their lives. In the case of therapeutic groups, these changes may be needed in order to ensure group members' physical and psychological well-being, or even survival (e.g. changes in relation to self-harming, eating disorders and drug/alcohol abuse). This may involve attending a number of sessions and ultimately may require referral to medical professionals. PLD group work, by contrast, focuses on the positive changes that young people can make in order to help them to achieve specific life goals and transitions (e.g. changes concerning decision making, assertiveness, job seeking). However, unlike therapeutic group work, PLD sessions do not set out to provide in-depth emotional or psychological support in a therapeutic context.

Finally, and probably most importantly, therapeutic groups and PLD sessions are likely to share a philosophy based on humanistic (or person-centred) principles (Rogers, 1965) that can be applied in both a therapeutic and an educational context. Both counsellors and facilitators, for the most part, believe that young people are best placed to make their own decisions. They also believe that young people have the resources at their disposal to make informed decisions and to plan and take action in relation to these, leading to positive change in their lives. However, where the work of a counsellor in a therapeutic context will be informed mainly by established counselling perspectives (e.g. cognitive behavioural therapy (Mennuti et al., 2006) or solution-focused approaches (de Shazer, 1994), the PLD facilitator will be drawing on a range of theoretical approaches (including learning theory, group dynamics and counselling concepts) to underpin their work with groups.

The case study detailed below provides an example of a therapeutic group session facilitated by a school counsellor.

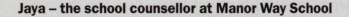

Jaya – the school counsellor at Manor Way School

Normally, Jaya's work is with individuals who have been referred by staff in the school (or by pupils themselves) when issues or concerns have arisen. However, recently a group of young people in the school has been identified as self-harming. Jaya has agreed to work with this group, providing them with a safe place in which to discuss their thoughts and feelings about what they are doing and why. At times these sessions can become very emotional as the young people share difficult and painful experiences with their peers.

Having examined teaching, informal education and therapeutic group work, a sense of the key features of personal learning and development group sessions delivered by youth support workers is beginning to emerge. Let us explore this further.

Personal learning and development: group work delivered by youth support workers in educational settings

The case study set out below provides an example of a PLD session delivered by a youth support worker in school.

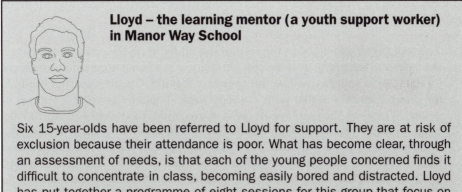

Lloyd – the learning mentor (a youth support worker) in Manor Way School

Six 15-year-olds have been referred to Lloyd for support. They are at risk of exclusion because their attendance is poor. What has become clear, through an assessment of needs, is that each of the young people concerned finds it difficult to concentrate in class, becoming easily bored and distracted. Lloyd has put together a programme of eight sessions for this group that focus on developing each member's concentration skills. The sessions are also aimed at raising self-esteem and confidence. Lloyd has structured the sessions with activities and input that will draw on the experience and expertise of group members. At the end of each session every group member will develop an action plan to work towards before they next meet.

It is clear that the personal and social issues facing many young people in education (which may include lack of confidence, experiencing low self-esteem, encountering barriers to opportunities, making decisions about their lives and experiencing difficulty in managing their behaviour) can be addressed to great effect in a group context. The purpose of PLD 'group work' is to attend to these personal issues, focusing on each *individual's personal and developmental needs*, but in a group setting. To state this in simple terms, the *young person* rather than a specific curriculum area or subject provides the focus for the PLD group. Gerrity and DeLucia-Waack describe PLD group work as 'psycho-educational/guidance groups', whereby young people work together in a group involving:

> Role-playing, problem-solving, decision-making, and communication skills training to teach specific skills and coping strategies in an effort to prevent problems (i.e. anger management, social skills, self-esteem, assertiveness, making friends.
> (Gerrity and DeLucia-Waack, 2007: 98)

Higgins and Westergaard (2001) define PLD sessions as 'guidance' group work, citing the activity of group work within the broader curriculum area of careers education and guidance. They acknowledge that delivering group work forms part of the role of the careers adviser, with topics such as 'decision making', 'choosing options', 'team building', 'preparing for transitions' and 'exploring occupations' being addressed in 'one-off' group sessions as part of a careers education and guidance programme. However, PLD sessions are increasingly being delivered outside the education curriculum as part of a larger integrated personal, social and health education strategy within schools. It is true to say, however, that Higgins and Westergaard describe with accuracy the key characteristics of guidance group work and these features can equally be applied to PLD sessions. They identify three underpinning principles:

1   The topic to be addressed in the session should focus on the *personal needs of the individuals* in the group. It is the responsibility of the facilitator to identify a topic for the session and they will set out to ensure that it will be relevant and useful to the group members at that time. Consideration should be given to a number of points: Where are the participants 'at' in terms of their personal and educational development? What are the key issues that may be around for them at this point in their lives? Is there a specific need (developmental, educational, emotional or behavioural) for this group of young people that could be addressed through group work? What might be the underpinning issues related to the topic? *In the previous case study, Lloyd is working with a small group of 15-year-old pupils to address their lack of concentration in the classroom. He has prepared a series of sessions that focus on the needs of this group. One of the sessions is entitled 'Developing Concentration Skills'.*

2   The session should include an opportunity for group members to focus and reflect on *their own position* in relation to the topic, otherwise known as 'What's in it for me?' Although the topic has been identified as being 'of use' and relevant to

a number of young people, each individual's response to it may be quite different. *For example, every young person in Lloyd's 'Developing Concentration Skills' session will have the opportunity to consider 'Why do I find concentrating hard?' and 'What gets in the way of me being able to concentrate?' and 'What might I do about it?'*

3   The session should consider the specific *action that each individual needs to take* in relation to the topic. It is not enough that the topic is discussed; underlying issues are explored and the session ends with a greater understanding for individuals within the group. Positive though this is, PLD group work goes further. Individuals within the session are helped to think about how they would like 'things to be different' and to identify specific actions that they can take as a result of the session to effect some change. *For example, the young people in the 'Developing Concentration Skills' session will have the opportunity not only to consider what the issues are for them in relation to the difficulties they experience in concentrating, but they will also make specific plans in relation to developing their own concentration skills. 'How am I going to change?' 'What do I need to do now?'*

The theory that supports PLD group work draws from a range of disciplines. Practitioners undertaking PLD sessions may be familiar with approaches and concepts underpinning education and learning (these are explored in some depth in Chapter 2), but they should also acknowledge skills and models that derive from other disciplines; for example, counselling and guidance. PLD facilitators are not teachers, although they may use knowledge of learning theory (Kolb, 1984; Gardner, 1993; Brandes and Ginnis, 1996) and group management techniques (Young, 2005) in their work. Neither are they counsellors, although they may use counselling skills and methods in order to build a rapport with the group (Westergaard, 2005). PLD facilitators perform a unique function with an emphasis that is different to teachers, informal educators and counsellors. However, PLD facilitators are skilled professionals who are clear about what they are setting out to achieve. Institutions in which youth support workers are employed should recognize and celebrate the fact that these practitioners are able to offer something unique and valuable to their pupils.

Summary

In this chapter, two key points have emerged. First, the job titles associated with youth support work are many and varied. However, there is a common link between the roles in that all youth support workers aim to assist young people to engage with their learning, manage their lives and achieve their aspirations. This is done using a range of techniques and interventions, one of which involves working with groups. Providing support to young people in a group context can have advantages over one-to-one interactions. The single most significant advantage is that there is an additional resource to be had in the shape of the group itself. By sharing feelings, thoughts, ideas and experiences with each other, young people can often be helped to find solutions to the problems they face and the decisions they need to make. By so doing, they can be enabled to manage their lives more effectively.

Table 1.1 A comparison of different group work sessions

	Personal learning and development	Teaching	Informal education (youth work)	Therapeutic groups
Purpose	To develop self-awareness and decision-making skills and make positive change	To gain knowledge, understanding and skills relating to an academic, creative or technical subject	To develop personal skills and abilities through interaction with others	To gain greater self-understanding, receive support and work towards change
Content	Based on an assessment of individual needs Interactive and experiential	Based on a curriculum/syllabus Range of teaching methods used	Based on developing skills in working together Project-driven	Determined by participants Sharing thoughts and feelings
Style of leadership	Facilitating	Managing the class	Leading by example Role-modelling	Counselling

Second, what has become evident is that the types of group session delivered by youth support workers are different to other, established forms of group activity. For example, where teachers focus on delivering a preset curriculum, youth support workers engage with the needs of the individual. Where informal educators develop the skills and qualities of group members by undertaking project work or informal learning opportunities, youth support workers deliver structured, time-bound sessions. Where counsellors focus on the in-depth emotional needs of their clients, youth support workers attend to social, behavioural and personal issues. Of course, youth support workers will draw on the theoretical concepts from the other disciplines to inform their work with groups, but they will also be clear that what they are offering young people is something quite different and of value in its own right.

Questions

The following questions will assist reflection on the key concepts introduced in this chapter.

1 **Identify the different elements of your own job role. How much of your work is focused on one-to-one support and how much involves working with groups?**

2 **Why do you work with groups of young people?**

3 **What can be achieved in a group that is less easily achieved by working one-to-one?**

4 **Identify the times when you have worked with groups of young people. What was the context in which the group was established?**

5 **What are the key features of PLD group work and how does it differ from teaching, informal education and therapeutic groups?**

2

Applying learning theory to personal learning and development group work

---

Learning Objectives

· Define experiential learning and its relevance to personal learning and development group work

· Examine key theories of learning

· Identify a range of learning styles

Introduction

As established in Chapter 1, the focus for group work facilitated by youth support workers will be on young people's personal learning and development (PLD). This learning may not relate to academic, creative or technical subject matter (e.g. history, drama, technology or sports studies), but will nevertheless involve participants in an active learning experience whereby the learning will focus on each group member's personal needs, development and decision making. As already stated, youth support workers in education settings may be facilitating PLD sessions on a range of topics, including self-awareness, assertiveness, anger management, stress management, option choices, decision-making skills, confidence building (the list goes on ...). Although these topics do not normally form part of an established curriculum area, they set out to help young people to learn about an aspect of 'self' (thoughts, feelings, experiences, choices, consequences and decisions) and to apply this learning outside the classroom and into their lives. It is therefore critical that those involved in delivering PLD group sessions understand the ways in which people learn.

This chapter begins by exploring two key theoretical frameworks. First, it focuses on the concept of experiential learning (Kolb, 1984). It examines how our reflections on the experiences we have (and the experiences of others) inform the ways in which we respond subsequently, having *learned by experience*. Second, it establishes the meaning of a 'person-centred' or, in the education context, a 'student-centred' approach to learning (Rogers, 1965). Student-centred learning emphasizes the uniqueness of individual learners and recognizes their potential and strengths in reflecting on, taking responsibility for, making decisions about, and engaging in, their own learning and development. Both theoretical approaches (experiential learning and student-centred concepts) are examined in the light of youth support work. In practical terms, this chapter demonstrates how knowledge of these two key learning theories can assist the youth support worker in planning and delivering PLD group sessions with young people.

The chapter then moves on to focus on a range of approaches to learning. Key education theorists have suggested that all individuals have particular strengths and preferences in relation to the way in which they learn (Entwistle, 1988; Gardner, 1993; Vermunt, 1994; Hermann, 1996; Myers and McCaulley, 1998; Honey and Mumford, 2000). These different aptitudes to learning are commonly termed *learning styles*, and two different, but related learning styles, are examined in this chapter. It is important, at this point, to be clear that there is little consensus about the validity of the concept of learning styles. A recent survey and evaluation of the literature proved inconclusive. It states, 'the field of learning styles consists of a wide variety of approaches that stem from different perspectives which have some underlying similarities and some conceptual overlap'. It goes on to suggest that 'research into learning styles can, in the main, be characterised as small-scale, non-cumulative, uncritical and inward-looking' (Coffield et al., 2004: 135).

However, although there is little hard evidence to support the existence of different learning styles, practitioners will be aware through their own experiences of learning, both in formal education and through personal and professional development opportunities, of the learning activities that suit them best. In their work with young people too, youth support professionals will see that there are identifiable differences in the way individuals engage with their learning. Some, for example, may learn most effectively by being involved in a range of practical activities, while others might prefer to observe and reflect. Similarly, some young people might learn by being given verbal instructions while others may prefer to read them. The concept of learning styles exists, has been embraced by many in the education professions and research is ongoing. However, as Pritchard summarizes:

> When all of the findings, however tentative some of them might be, are considered together, and when some of the assumptions from research are tested and re-examined in more detail, we are able to arrive at a generally accepted set of approaches to teaching which seem to be effective. This set of approaches is wide, variable and constantly shifting. That is to say, there is not a one-size-fits-all answer to the questions 'How do children learn?' and 'How should teachers teach?'
>
> (Pritchard, 2005: viii)

Before examining the theories and concepts that underpin learning, it is helpful to attempt to establish what learning is and how we can provide evidence that it has taken place.

What is learning?

As already suggested, what learning means, how learning takes place and how it is measured, is an ongoing discourse where every attempt at definition is systematically contested. It is not the purpose of this book to enter that debate, but it is important to recognize that for PLD group work to be effective, personal learning should take place; and if learning is to take place, we need to know what it might look like and what enables it to happen. The scenarios outlined below provide a useful starting point in considering the meaning of learning in practice.

James – a 16-year-old pupil at Manor Way School

James is studying for his end of school examinations and one of his subjects is maths. James finds maths a struggle, and he is challenged, in particular, by a formula he has to use in order to understand and solve problems. James has been shown how to use the formula by his teacher on numerous occasions and he is aware of the steps that he needs to take in order to get an answer. Sometimes he arrives at the correct answer to the problems set, sometimes he doesn't. In either case, he is not clear about what he might have done that is right or wrong.

Question
Has James *learned and understood* what he is doing and why he is doing it?

Natasha – a 15-year-old pupil at Manor Way School

Natasha is captain of the school basketball team. She has developed skills, knowledge and techniques in relation to playing the game of basketball and furthermore she is aware of the rules of basketball and how these will have a practical impact on the game. Her teacher has helped her to develop these skills and has enabled her to think strategically about the game she is playing. Natasha is able to share her knowledge and skills with her team mates.

Question
Has Natasha *learned and understood* what she is doing and why?

Tariq – a 14-year-old pupil at Manor Way School

Tariq is very keen to be involved in drama. He has joined the drama club and he has been selected to play a key part in the next production, which is a Shakespeare play. Tariq takes a copy of the play home with him and in one week, by repeating his lines over and over, he has memorized one of his speeches. He is word perfect, but he has little awareness of the plot and hasn't developed an understanding of his character and others in the play.

Question
Has Tariq *learned and understood* what he is saying and why he is saying it?

Emma – a 15-year-old pupil at Manor Way School

Emma has been excluded from her lessons on a number of occasions for being disruptive. The pattern is always the same. As far as she is concerned, she and her friends are equally disruptive in class. They chat and giggle and are often disengaged from their work. However, it is Emma who is usually the one excluded. She feels 'picked on' by her teachers and thinks that it is unfair that she is the student who is sent out of the room. After a 'cooling-off' period, Emma is invited to rejoin the class, but inevitably the pattern will repeat itself.

Question
Has Emma *learned and understood* why she is being excluded?

In the scenarios outlined above, it is likely that although James, Tariq and Emma have been told about or shown how to do something, they each, at this stage, have very little understanding of what they are doing and why they are doing it. Natasha, on the other hand, is able to demonstrate her application of skills and knowledge in relation to the game of basketball. To the observer, Natasha's play may seem effortless or even instinctive; however, it has developed to this level because Natasha has engaged with a learning process. To learn then requires an element of understanding. Knowing not simply what we are doing, but why and how we are doing it is central to learning. For example, if James understood why and how the formula for solving mathematical problems worked, he would feel more prepared to tackle complex problem-solving tasks. He would use the formula confidently, knowing and understanding what he is doing, why it is working and how he could do things differently if need be. Similarly, if Tariq had a greater understanding of the play, the characters in it, the relationships between them, the language, the narrative and the themes, he would know and understand the meaning behind the words and as a result he would be able to deliver his lines with confidence and appropriate emphasis.

Emma's case is particularly interesting as it is likely that at some point she will be referred to a youth support worker for additional help to address the issue of her behaviour in the classroom. Emma needs support in order to enable her to understand her behaviour, to identify what triggers the behaviour and to explore what she can do differently to ensure a happier outcome. Emma has not yet learned enough about herself to enable her to make changes to her behaviour in the classroom. It is likely to be a central aspect of the role of the youth support professional who works with Emma, to help her to know and understand more about her behaviour and how it can be managed effectively. Each of the scenarios outlined above involve the development of learning. But it is only Emma's scenario that focuses specifically on the learning with which youth support workers are concerned: developing knowledge and understanding about 'self'.

These case studies provide us with practical examples of what learning is and what it is not. Arnold and Yeomans offer a concise definition of learning that reflects and clarifies what we have discovered when considering James, Natasha, Tariq and Emma's situations:

> One thing that all the theories do have in common is the view that learning involves some kind of change. Common sense tells us that after we have learned something we have changed in some way. For example, we add to our repertoire of facts about something that interests us, or we are able to perform a skill such as driving or knitting that we could not do before.
>
> (Arnold and Yeomans, 2004: 102)

This definition resonates clearly with PLD group work delivered by youth support workers, where a key aim is to enable change through greater understanding. This change may be related to knowledge, behaviour, attitudes or skills, and evidence that a change has taken place should exist. For example, if Emma understands why she becomes easily distracted in class, and if she learns strategies to enable her to deal with this more effectively in her lessons, then the change will be clear for all to see. Emma will be less distracted and more engaged in her work.

So, if learning involves understanding and working towards change, what are the learning theories that can help youth support workers to plan group work sessions providing opportunities for young people to learn?

Experiential learning

One of the most influential concepts to have developed in education is that of experiential learning (Dewey, 1938; Lewin, 1951; Piaget, 1971; Kolb, 1984). The term 'experiential learning' is, in many ways, self-explanatory. Clearly, it refers to the need for individuals to experience something and to learn from the experience. For learning to take place, individuals will need to reflect on the experience they have had, to make sense of it and to consider what they would do differently if they were to have a similar experience in the future. They would then act on this when the opportunity arose. For example, if children go out on a cold morning without gloves, their hands go numb and they feel discomfort or even pain. On the next cold day they will think back to their previous experience, remember how it felt, decide that this was not a good feeling and will act by putting gloves in their pocket when they go out. This is a very simple example of experiential learning, but the same theory can be applied to more sophisticated learning tasks. Miller and Boud explain this clearly:

> When we learn, we engage in a complex process which draws on the behaviour, knowledge and skills of people around us as well as on the material and infor- mational resources of the world we live in, such as bus timetables, library books, television programmes and the internet. But we also use and build upon our own

personal foundation of experience. Our learning is grounded in prior experience. It is profoundly influenced by this experience as well as the context in which we operate.

(Miller and Boud, 1996: 3)

The concept of experiential learning can be illustrated further in the case study below.

Claire – a 15-year-old pupil at Manor Way School

Claire travels to school on the bus with her best friend Michelle. Every day, Michelle is delayed and both girls often miss the bus and are late for school, thus incurring detentions. Claire has decided that she will not wait for Michelle any longer in the mornings as she doesn't want to be late for school and punished for something that is not her fault. Simply put – Claire has learned by her experience and has changed her behaviour accordingly.

In the example above, Claire has learned through her own direct experience with Michelle. However, it is important to be aware that the concept of experiential learning does not mean that we must experience a situation ourselves in order to learn from it. Claire could equally have learned by hearing about someone else's similar situation. If, for example, a mutual friend, upset and angry, had talked to Claire about her own experiences when waiting for Michelle, explaining that she had been in trouble for being late when she was not to blame, Claire may have decided at the outset not to wait for her friend. By finding out about, or observing the experiences of others, it is possible to reflect on and relate these to our own situation, thus learning (and change) has taken place.

Kolb (1984) developed a model that illustrates clearly the cyclical and ongoing nature of learning by experience. Reynolds argues; 'Kolb's cycle has struck a chord with educators wanting to relate learning to experience and, as a result, has been very influential with those practising group work and other experiential methods' (Reynolds, 1994: 31). The model is illustrated in Figure 2.1.

The model can also be used as a framework (Figure 2.2) when planning activities in PLD group sessions as seen in Chapter 5.

It is important therefore for youth support workers to understand the significance that experience plays in learning, and to structure learning experiences into PLD sessions by encouraging young people to share, reflect on, evaluate and learn from their own situations and those of others. Chapter 5 examines this in more detail.

The second key learning theory that underpins PLD group work is that of student-centred learning.

Student-centred learning

Many youth support workers will be familiar with the concept of person-centred approaches (Rogers, 1965) in their one-to-one work with young people. They will be

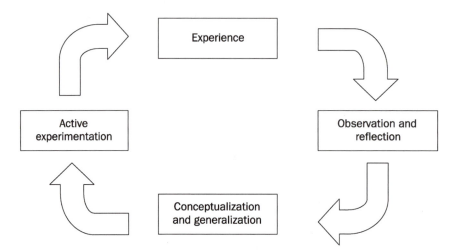

Figure 2.1 Kolb's experiential learning cycle
Source: Kolb (1984)

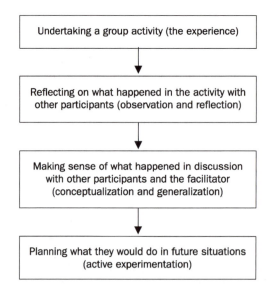

Figure 2.2 Experiential learning as a framework for group activity

aware of the importance of adhering to person-centred principles which, in brief, suggest that:

- we are all unique;
- we are all born 'good' with a drive to develop to our full potential or 'self-actualize';

- we each have the resources for personal growth;
- we are best placed to take responsibility for, and make decisions about, our lives;
- we may experience barriers to self-actualization;
- we may need help in overcoming the barriers that have constrained our development.

Although youth support workers will be familiar with the concept of person-centred approaches, they may, however, be less clear about how these principles can be applied to the education context, where person-centred becomes student-centred. Brandes and Ginnis provide a full and helpful explanation of what student-centred learning means:

> The ownership of learning is with the student. The teacher acts as a facilitator and a resource-person. Students are responsible for choosing and planning the curriculum, or at least they participate in the choosing. Learning is self-initiated, and often involves the processes of enquiry and discovery; the learner is also responsible for evaluating the results. A difficult concept to grasp, at first, is that each individual is 100% responsible for his own behaviour, participation and learning.
>
> (Brandes and Ginnis, 1996: 12)

Of course, there may be those who find the concept of student-centred learning daunting (Scruton, 1987). For example, taken literally, this approach would require teachers to consult their students about the curriculum in order to decide whether or not they value it as being of relevance. This may provide a particular challenge for a teacher of geography or science for example, but, by contrast, it offers an opportunity to the youth support worker who is working with a group of young people to identify and address their needs. By assessing the needs of the young people in the group and by focusing on their personal learning and development issues, student-centred learning principles are being adhered to. Arnold and Yeomans develop this point further:

> Where in the system is there room for learning based on personal needs, self-direction and facilitation rather than on teaching? Perhaps we should consider the interpersonal emphasis in Rogers' approach. Despite the imposition of curriculum content, teaching methodology and external performance benchmarks, the essence of teaching still involves interaction between an adult and a group of children or young people.
>
> (Arnold and Yeomans, 2004: 138)

The student-centred approach to learning emphasizes the relationship between learner and facilitator. This emphasis on relationship building will resonate with youth support practitioners. A core element of their work, both one-to-one and in groups, is taking time to establish relationships of trust with young people. Furthermore, unlike other subject areas in the curriculum, PLD group work is based on the needs of the individual. Therefore, if group members can be encouraged to engage with the topic, to see that it is relevant to them at this point in time and to want to understand more about it (and themselves) in order to make change in their lives – then they will be motivated to take an active part. The example below illustrates the concept of student-centred learning in youth support practice.

Lloyd – the learning mentor in Manor Way School

Lloyd has been asked to work with a group of eight pupils who have recently experienced family breakdown. This is having an impact on their learning in class and they have been identified as exhibiting 'challenging' behaviour with teachers and their peers. If Lloyd is to work effectively with this group, he must ensure that he has engaged with them and established a rapport. He must also encourage them to be willing and active participants in the sessions. This may mean spending time with the group, establishing what they need from the sessions and reaching agreement about topics that it would be useful to cover. By so doing, Lloyd is acknowledging that the young people have the capacity to take responsibility for their learning and are best placed to make decisions about what it is they need in order to effect change. Lloyd is adhering to and putting into practice student-centred learning principles by treating the group as individuals with a shared issue (family breakdown) but with their own responses to the issue. By encouraging group members to take responsibility for decision making about their learning, Lloyd is not imposing his own ideas about what is 'best' for the young people in the group.

In order to work in a truly student-centred way, youth support workers should be encouraged to demonstrate the use of three core conditions (Rogers, 1965) that will enable individual group members to feel valued, to take responsibility for their learning and to achieve greater self-awareness. These core conditions are:

- Empathy – working hard to understand the 'whole person'. Trying to establish the frame of reference of individual group members. What is going on in their life? How does it feel to be in their position?
- Congruence – being 'real' and genuine in the relationship with the group. Not 'playing the part' of a facilitator, but being an active, engaged and open member of the group
- Unconditional positive regard – accepting that all members of the group are individuals with a right to their own opinions, beliefs, and values (informed by their life experiences). It is not necessary to agree with, or even like the group members, but a non-judgemental approach is important to establishing understanding and building rapport.

Youth support workers who use these core conditions in their one-to-one practice will know that adhering to them can be demanding. The group context provides an additional challenge. The youth support worker delivering PLD sessions will be engaging not only with individual learners, but also with the relationships between group members and the dynamic of the group itself. This is neither simple nor straightforward; however, youth support workers who maintain a student-centred approach in their work will find that young people in the group are likely to flourish and learn.

So far, this chapter has looked at two distinct, but related theories of learning. The first of these is experiential learning, which proposes that learning takes place as a result of having an experience, reflecting on it, making sense of it and putting new strategies into practice in the future. The second, student-centred learning, emphasizes the importance of enabling young people to engage in their learning and take responsibility for it, while paying particular attention to the relationship that develops between the facilitator and group members. In addition to these two key theoretical perspectives, another concept of which the youth support worker should be aware is that of learning styles.

As explained at the start of this chapter, there is no clear consensus about the significance (or even the existence) of individual learning preferences. There is, however, an awareness of the concept of learning styles in many education institutions, and a recognition of the significance of learning styles by both policy makers and practitioners. It is therefore an important development that should be addressed in this book. The chapter examines the concept of learning styles in general and two different approaches to learning styles (or learning preferences) in particular.

Learning styles

The concept of learning styles came to prominence in the latter half of the twentieth century. There is general acknowledgement among those who are involved in helping individuals to learn that we learn in a variety of ways. The example below illustrates this clearly.

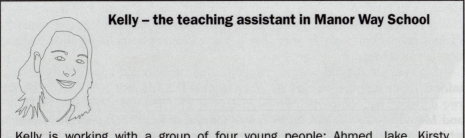

Kelly – the teaching assistant in Manor Way School

Kelly is working with a group of four young people: Ahmed, Jake, Kirsty and Amy. These students have been identified as lacking concentration in class and are often disruptive. Kelly has been asked by the head of year to take these students for a one-hour PLD session once a week to work on developing their concentration skills. Kelly has discovered the following:

Ahmed: has lots of energy and takes an active part in anything that involves 'doing'. He always makes positive contributions and learns most from the PLD session when he is involved in an activity, particularly one that demands a hands-on approach. He struggles with activities where he is required to sit quietly and read, or listen to Kelly talking about something. He switches off, becomes distracted and starts to disrupt other group members.

Jake: appears very quiet and withdrawn in the group. He contributes little to discussions and often seems disinterested and disengaged. However, Kelly was surprised to discover how involved Jake became when she asked the group to make a collage that expressed what they felt when they were in lessons with teachers. Jake produced an amazing piece of work, which he was comfortable to talk about with others in the group. Following the activity, Jake shared surprise at what he had learned about his feelings, and the impact they had on his behaviour.

Kirsty: often appears lethargic. Her constant mantra is 'what's the point in doing this'. Kelly has discovered that when Kirsty *can* see 'the point' she becomes animated and engaged in the session. She is willing to take a lead and helps to motivate others in the group and she is keen to think about ways in which her learning can be applied in her life outside the PLD group.

Amy: struggles with reading and writing. She will become 'switched off' by any activity that involves using these skills. She will walk around the room and start distracting others. Kelly was pleasantly surprised to find that when she asked the group to compose a song with the title 'Concentration', Amy was keen to write the lyrics and took an active part in finding words that could be expressed to music.

By working with this small group, Kelly has realized that each young person has strengths in relation to learning, and each is motivated to learn in different ways. Not only has this had an impact on how effectively young people engage with the PLD sessions, but Kelly is sure that it has wider implications on their learning throughout school.

So, what are the different learning styles and how might knowing about them
\rm youth support practice in group work? This chapter goes on to examine
different, but complementary perspectives. The first was developed by Honey
umford (2000), and draws heavily on the concept of experiential learning,
\s discussed earlier in the chapter. The second is Gardner's (1993) theory of
telligences. Both approaches are established within the literature, and can
ful insight, while neither has been proven to offer a definitive guide to the
individuals learn.

Honey and Mumford's learning styles

Honey and Mumford identified four different preferences to learning. Each of these learning preferences, or styles, relates to an element of Kolb's learning cycle, thereby suggesting that individuals have a tendency to gain most learning at key times in the experiential learning process. However, Honey and Mumford assert that although there are four key learning styles (one for each stage in the experiential learning process), most of us possess one or two preferred, or dominant, learning styles. They developed a questionnaire which, when completed, provides an indication of which learning style is strongest and which is less dominant in an individual. The four learning styles are set out below and the link to the stage of Kolb's learning cycle is made:

- Activist – someone who needs to be involved in learning, taking an active part, quick to join in, keen to 'have the experience'. However, the activist can become easily bored, quickly distracted and want to move on (Kolb's experiential learning cycle: *experience*).

- Reflector – someone who takes time to think something through, to 'put it under the microscope' and examine it in detail. Reflectors may not be the first to 'join in' with an activity; they may be reluctant or even appear disinterested (Kolb's experiential learning cycle: *observation and reflection*).

- Theorist – someone who needs to understand the theoretical or conceptual basis for something. Why does this happen? Who says so? How do we know that there is not another way of looking at things? Theorists will enjoy using research skills, but, like reflectors, may find it difficult to join in activities (Kolb's experiential learning cycle: *conceptualization and generalization*).

- Pragmatist – someone who is motivated to engage with learning as long as it is of value, has a point and is purposeful. They look for practical solutions, always keen to apply their learning. A session that appears pointless and irrelevant will not stimulate the pragmatist (Kolb's experiential learning cycle: *active experimentation*).

Ideally, in order to maximize their learning potential, learners should have the capacity to access or 'tap into' each of the four learning styles at any given time, depending on the situation. However, as already stated, in reality most of us have one or two dominant learning styles and are less able to access others. This may prove problematic if we are not provided with opportunities to learn that will suit our own learning styles (this is investigated further in Chapter 5). Alternatively, it is helpful to try to develop those learning styles that are less dominant in order to maximize our learning potential. Pritchard sums this up helpfully:

Each individual will adopt an approach to learning with which they are most comfortable, and in doing so leave behind the approaches with which they are less comfortable. It is helpful for learners if they are aware of their own particular learning preferences in order that they can use an appropriate learning style to suit the particular activity that is being undertaken, and take opportunities to improve their potential for learning when faced with a learning activity that might steer them towards one of their 'weaker' – or at least one of their less favoured – styles.

(Pritchard, 2005: 55)

So, to return to Kelly's group where students have been selected as needing help with developing concentration skills, it may be that Ahmed is displaying activist learning style tendencies that can be misinterpreted as a lack of concentration. In fact, it could simply be the case that Ahmed learns best by taking an *activist* approach, and Kelly needs to take this into consideration when she is planning the PLD sessions. Fellow group member Kirsty, who needs to know 'what's the point' of the session and the activities, may be indicating a *pragmatist* learning style. Perhaps if the purpose of the session and the outcomes of each activity are made clear and relevant to her, Kirsty may engage more readily. However, Honey and Mumford's learning styles do not, at first glance, appear to offer any significant insight into either Jake or Amy's learning preference. So, are there other approaches to learning that may help Kelly to develop her understanding of how Jake and Amy can be helped to learn more effectively?

Gardner's multiple intelligences

Gardner (1993) may be able to provide Kelly with some insight into Jake and Amy's preferred approach to learning. He has drawn from the fields of neurobiology, anthropology and psychology in order to inform his thinking about ways in which individuals learn. His basic premise is that intelligence is not fixed, but is comprised of a range of seven aptitudes that can be developed. Although individuals are born with all seven of these 'intelligences', it is likely that, like Honey and Mumford's learning styles, some of these will develop and become dominant, or preferred, while others are used little or not at all. The seven intelligences are listed below:

1   Linguistic – good with the written word, learns most effectively through reading, telling stories and enjoys writing thoughts and feelings down.
2   Mathematical/logical – problem-solvers, aptitude for numbers, logical, can think through a sequence of ideas.
3   Visual/spatial – good at visualizing and imagining, able to construct three-dimensional objects, awareness of, and sound judgement in using space.
4   Musical – enjoy music and have a good sense of rhythm, moods easily affected by music, enjoy playing a musical instrument.
5   Interpersonal – able to see different points of view, maintain a range of relationships and learn from sharing with others, able to empathize with how others are feeling.
6   Intrapersonal – aware of own thoughts and feelings and a need for an explanation of them, accurate self-concept, strong values and beliefs, keen to learn and develop.
7   Kinaesthetic – good control and use of the body, learning by 'doing', need to be physically active.

Gardner is clear that it is likely for a variety of reasons that most individuals do not develop equally in all seven intelligences. Smith explains:

> Gardner believes that each intelligence is modifiable and can be expanded. There are predictable factors such as cultural influences in and around the home. As the senses are activated and cellular connections are made throughout childhood, so the intelligence is developed. The more stimulation the more the development.
>
> (Smith, 1996: 53)

So, how can knowledge of Gardner's multiple intelligences help Kelly, the teaching assistant, to plan PLD sessions with Ahmed, Kirsty, Jake and Amy more effectively? Youth support workers who are aware of these different aptitudes to learning will be able to think creatively about the use of a range of activities that will promote learning. For example, in the PLD group work outlined earlier in the chapter, where the topic focuses on developing concentration skills, Kelly could offer a range of activities to encourage the young people to identify their own barriers to concentration. She could provide a 'menu' from which students select an activity that most appeals to their learning preference. The menu could include:

- Individually list and reflect on the situations in which concentration is a challenge (linguistic, intrapersonal, mathematical/logical).
- List and reflect on the barriers in pairs (interpersonal, linguistic, mathematical/logical).
- Present the barriers to concentration in visual form – either a picture or a model (spatial/visual, kinaesthetic).
- Prepare a piece of drama or dance that demonstrates the barriers (musical, kinaesthetic).
- Write a song that has 'barriers to concentration' as its title (musical, linguistic, intrapersonal, interpersonal if done in pairs or groups).

By providing a choice for learners, Kelly can be sure that all group members will have the opportunity to work to their strengths. Clearly, it is not always practical or possible to structure PLD sessions in such a way that a range of activities are offered from which young people select, based on their preferred learning style. However, by having an awareness that individuals learn in different ways, youth support workers can ensure that they use a variety of activities, methods of delivery and learning techniques in their sessions. This will ensure that all group members have the opportunity to maximize their learning potential. It will also minimize the risk that individuals are left to struggle or are marginalized within the group because the activities planned do not resonate with their preferred learning style.

There is an important final point to be made on learning styles that is explored in more detail in Chapter 5. Facilitators should ensure that they have a clear understanding of their own learning preference. There is a danger, when planning activities, for youth support workers (consciously or unconsciously) to select the methods of delivery that most closely reflect their own learning style. This may mean that they inadvertently exclude group members who do not share this particular preference for learning.

Summary

This chapter has focused on the concept of learning. It has established a definition of learning as it applies to PLD work, emphasizing the importance of learning about *self* in order to understand and work towards meeting individual needs. The two central approaches to learning that have been explored are experiential learning and student-centred learning. These approaches can be integrated by practitioners by recognizing that students learn by experience and providing these experiences in sessions, while at the same time acknowledging the need for students to play an active part in, and take responsibility for, their own learning.

The chapter has also examined the concept of learning styles. While accepting that there is not general agreement about the significance of learning preferences, it is important to recognize that all young people have their own way of engaging with learning opportunities. By understanding this, youth support workers are encouraged to be flexible in their planning of PLD group sessions in order to ensure that every young person's needs are addressed.

Questions

The following questions will assist reflection on the key concepts introduced.

1 What do you understand 'learning' to mean in the context of PLD sessions?
2 How might the concept of experiential learning help you to plan your PLD sessions?
3 How student-centred is your group work with young people? How effectively do you adhere to the core conditions?
4 How does it help you to know that young people have different strengths in learning?
5 Reflect on group work that you have undertaken. What learning styles were evident in the group?

3
Assessing needs and identifying a topic

Learning Objectives
- Describe the personal learning and development needs of a range of young people
- Identify topics for PLD sessions
- Analyse ways in which PLD sessions will meet the needs of a range of young people

Introduction

So far, this book has established the role of a range of youth support workers and has outlined a definition of personal learning and development group work. It has also examined key theoretical concepts underpinning the experience of learning. By exploring the various ways in which young people learn, youth support workers should be better equipped to plan, prepare and facilitate PLD sessions for students.

In this chapter the focus shifts from the abstract and conceptual, to the more practical. An approach to planning and preparing PLD group work is examined and the FAAST model (Westergaard, 2007) is introduced.

This model has been developed to provide youth support workers with a framework for constructing, preparing and delivering PLD sessions. It suggests a chronology for planning which, if followed, will ensure that PLD sessions are well structured. This will provide maximum opportunities for learning by using a range of appropriate activities and techniques. The acronym 'FAAST' stands for:

- Focus
- Aim
- Activities
- Structure
- Techniques

This book is structured in such a way as to follow the chronology of the FAAST model, chapter by chapter. It begins in this chapter by examining the Focus of the session by exploring the needs of young people and identifying topics, which will enable them to address and meet these needs. In subsequent chapters the Aim, Activities, Structure and Techniques are examined.

To ensure that an appropriate focus (or topic) is identified, youth support workers should engage first with a process of assessing needs. This involves identifying a range of personal learning and development issues that young people may have at various points in their lives and from an assessment of these, selecting an appropriate topic (or focus) for the session. The chapter begins by identifying a range of needs that may be shared by young people at particular times in their development. It examines the internal and external factors that impact on young people, including their physical, emotional, social and educational development. Furthermore, it emphasizes the ways in which PLD sessions can encourage young people to manage these factors effectively, as they make various transitions through education and beyond. This is not as straightforward as it may at first appear. As Payne explains:

> The trouble is that what appears as a relatively straightforward process is much more complex when applied to real life. We cannot always see clearly what a 'need' is and others may have a different view.
>
> (Payne, 2005: 133)

Concrete and specific examples of 'needs' are provided in this chapter in order to establish their nature, and to consider how youth support workers can make accurate assessments of them. This process is central for informing the choice of PLD topic. Finally, a range of topics for PLD sessions are identified. Links are made between the needs that young people experience at particular times in their lives and the topics that youth support workers can address in PLD sessions.

The FAAST model

Youth support workers who undertake group work as a regular activity will be aware of the importance of ensuring that not only is the session engaging and interesting, but it also retains a sense of purpose and leads to positive learning outcomes for the young people involved. Higgins and Westergaard (2001) make the point that group work can strive so hard to be exciting, fun and 'different' from other activities in education that it risks losing a sense of direction and purpose. The FAAST model has been devised to ensure that PLD sessions are purposeful, structured and meet the needs of the young people participating in the group. In brief, the model is as follows:

- Focus – identifying an appropriate focus or topic for the session, based on an accurate assessment of the personal learning and development needs of the young people.
- Aim – ensuring that an aim for the session is identified and clearly stated. This will provide a sense of purpose for the session. Linked to the aim, learning

objectives will also be specified. It is the learning objectives that provide a clear indication as to what the session will achieve for the participants.

- Activities – planning activities that are relevant to the topic, address the aim of the session and meet the learning objectives. Activities should be selected carefully, paying attention to the diverse nature of the individuals within the group. Recognition of young people's different learning styles should also be apparent through the range of activities used.

- Structure – creating a structure for the session in order that the PLD group work provides and builds on a range of learning experiences for the young people involved. It is crucial that the session is much more than a series of activities; at best loosely held together by a thin thread; at worst totally disconnected. The session should offer clarity and coherence to the learners by providing a logical and rational structure through which they can progress.

- Techniques – finally, once the Focus for the session has been identified, the Aim agreed, the Activities planned and the Structure developed, the youth support worker will be engaged in the group session using a range of Techniques and skills to facilitate learning.

Often, youth support workers will find themselves planning their group sessions with the Activities as the starting point and only a very general sense of Focus for the session with little in the way of a specified Aim and objectives. This is often done with the best of intentions. First, it may be that the youth support worker has used an activity in a different PLD session, which has worked well in the past. They want to 'fit it in' to subsequent group work, finding a way to use the activity even if it is not particularly appropriate to the topic. Second, it may be because once the activities for the session are decided, the youth support worker will feel that most of the preparation is complete. When under pressure (as many youth support professionals are), this may present a comforting option. Third, it could be that youth support workers start their planning with designing activities because they have had little experience or training in delivering group work and are unaware that there is a chronological order to the planning process. Where the focus for the session is not decided at the outset, the session is likely to be messy and unstructured, lacking a clear sense of direction and unlikely to achieve positive learning outcomes for the young people involved. The FAAST framework can help reduce these risks. By expressing the model in diagrammatic form as seen in Figure 3.1, the chronology of the process becomes clear.

It is important to be aware that FAAST does not = 'fast'. It should not be assumed that the FAAST model is in any way a short cut to planning PLD sessions. It is, however, an efficient and meaningful way to ensure that PLD sessions are planned and delivered effectively.

Focus

Youth support workers, as a central feature of their role, will be working with young people in order to assess their needs and enable them to find strategies to meet these needs. In many cases, this work is undertaken on a one-to-one basis by building up

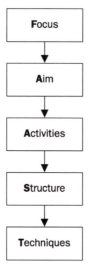

Figure 3.1 A chronology for planning, preparing and delivering PLD group work

relationships with the young people to a point where they feel comfortable to talk about the issues and concerns that they are facing. The work does not involve youth support practitioners in providing answers, 'telling someone what to do' or knowing 'what is best'; neither would be appropriate or, more importantly, helpful in encouraging young people to take responsibility for their own decision making. Instead, the work concentrates on enabling each young person to understand their situation better, think about strategies for making change and planning action steps to enable this to happen. The same is true of PLD sessions. The needs of the young people in the group are paramount, and the purpose of the session is to enable group members to explore their needs and identify ways forward. However, there is one key difference between one-to-one work and PLD group work. In one-to-one work, the youth support worker will not necessarily know what the needs of the young person are until they begin to discuss them. In PLD sessions, where youth support workers may be engaging with groups of up to 30 young people, it would not be practical or possible to facilitate the session without having identified a topic and planned activities to enable learning.

The youth support professional who starts the PLD session by asking the group, 'How do you want to use the session today?' is likely to find that there are as many responses as there are group members! Therefore, unlike one-to-one interactions, the youth support worker should engage with groups of young people, having first identified a clear focus for each session.

Assessing need

The importance of assessing the perceived needs of group members in order to identify an appropriate topic for PLD sessions should not be underestimated. Geldard and Geldard emphasize this point:

Careful programme planning followed by an effective assessment procedure is essential to ensure a successful group experience with the achievement of identified goals. Outcomes may be severely compromised if the assessment process does not carefully tease out important factors that need to be identified.

(Geldard and Geldard, 2001: 83)

The role of the youth support worker therefore is to begin planning the group session by establishing, *in general terms*, the possible issues that may be facing a group of young people at a particular point in their development. This assessment should take into account a number of factors including the gender, cultural, socio-economic and ethnic backgrounds of the young people. Once possible issues or needs are established, the youth support worker can begin to think in more detail about the specific group of young people, to identify and assess the issues and needs as they relate to this group. From this more in-depth assessment, the youth support worker will identify a focus for the session that aims to address the needs of all group members, although individuals within the group will have their own experiences and responses to it.

Of course, this identification and assessment of need assumes that the youth support worker has complete freedom and control with regard to the planning of group work. As many will be aware, this is often not the case. It may well be that youth support workers are asked by teachers or heads of year to work with a group of young people who have been identified as having a particular need. Alternatively, they may be invited to deliver a session as part of an existing programme (e.g. PHSE), in which case the 'assessment of need' is likely to have been undertaken by others. Where this happens the youth support worker is tasked with translating general preset topics into meaningful and relevant sessions that meet the needs of the group concerned.

So, how do youth support workers identify, in general terms, the needs of young people? Malekoff provides a helpful starting point, explaining that there are key developmental factors that have an impact on all young people. He states:

Regardless of any argument concerning the chronological onset of adolescence or social influences that affect developing children, there is universal agreement that 'developmental tasks' necessary for adolescents in our culture to become healthy, functioning adults requires great effort and time to achieve.

(Malekoff, 2004: 6)

He goes on to describe the four developmental tasks as:

1   breaking away and separating from the family;
2   establishing and accepting a healthy sexual identity;
3   considering and planning for the future;
4   becoming increasingly aware and developing beliefs through a moral value system.

Harper supports this view. He argues:

> The central development task of the young person is emancipation from parents. Issues of identity re-emerge and value structures are refined, as the lifestyle of the individual becomes increasingly established.
>
> (Harper, 1993: 69)

It is also important to be aware that the changes that take place in adolescence are not only significant, but happen in a relatively short time span. This can be a confusing and frightening place for young people to find themselves. Bee and Boyd explain that:

> It makes sense to divide the period from age 12 to age 20 into two sub-periods, one beginning at 12 or 13 and the other beginning at about 16. The first period, early adolescence, is marked by change in every area of development – physical changes, new educational demands, new social expectations. The young teen's main goal, from a developmental perspective is to make it through this period without becoming ensnared in one of the many possible negative patterns – drug use, delinquency, early sexual activity, and so forth – any of which can derail the identity development process.
>
> (Bee and Boyd, 2002: 336)

At this point, it is important to acknowledge the possible presence of a politically motivated agenda, which may emphasize the need to reduce the potential 'problems' created by young people as they develop through adolescence (Williamson, 2005). Policy makers will be all too aware of the significance of guiding young people and, in some cases, 'controlling' their behaviour, to ensure that they are able to make a positive contribution to society. Education institutions therefore have a role in enabling their students to meet social and educational targets now, which will translate into economic targets in the future. As a result, youth support workers may find themselves working with young people who have been identified by others as needing help with 'improving behaviour' or becoming 'more mature'. The young people may not perceive that there is a problem at all. This can provide the youth support worker with a challenge. The translation of strategic or policy priorities into ones that allow for student-centred learning principles requires youth support workers to pay attention to the planning and delivery of their PLD sessions and to be skilled in building meaningful relationships with groups of young people.

Table 3.1 builds on Malekoff's four developmental tasks by identifying different age groups and considering, in general terms, the kinds of issue that may impact on young people at each age and stage of their development. It does not set out to suggest that all young people experience the same physical, emotional, social and educational factors at the same time, but it does make clear that common features are likely to exist.

Of course, Table 3.1 does not provide a full and comprehensive list of the many and various factors that have an impact at each stage of young people's development. For example, social factors like housing, parenting or caring, relationships with

Table 3.1 Factors affecting young people's development

Age	Physical/emotional development factors	Social factors	Educational/transition factors
13–14	• Adolescence • Onset of puberty • Weight gain/loss • Change in body shape • Awareness of transition from childhood to adulthood • Sexual awareness and development • Need to rebel • Mood swings; autonomy to dependence • Lack of confidence • Lack of self-esteem	• Influence of peer group • Significance of friendships • Bullying • Isolation • Less dependence on parents/carers • Greater freedom • Experimentation with drugs/alcohol • Influence of role models • Struggle for identity • Opinions informed by stereotypes	• Subject option choices • Expectation by others of increased personal responsibility for learning • Increased homework tasks • Awareness of the significance of impending examinations
15–16	• Progress towards physical and sexual maturity • Greater confidence/lack of confidence • Increased awareness of self • Feelings of invincibility • Feeling out of control • Lack of energy/lethargy • Need for autonomy • Gender differences (physical emotional and behavioural become more pronounced) • Eating disorders/self-harming • Increased ability to make rational and informed decisions	• Continuing influence of peer group • Relationships with the opposite/same sex • Sexual experimentation • Clearer identity • Conflict with parents/carers • Acting out rebellious feelings • Risk taking • Criminal activity and other destructive behaviours may emerge • Disregard for authority	• Working towards examinations • Stress in relation to course work or exams • Need for information about options after compulsory schooling • Decisions about transitions • Fear about next steps • Apathy about next steps • Uncertainty about where to go to for help • Applications for further education, training or work • Part-time work (weekends or evenings)

(Continued overleaf)

Table 3.1 continued

Age	Physical/emotional development factors	Social factors	Educational/transition factors
17–19	• Close to physical and emotional maturity • Fear of future as an adult • Greater autonomy in decision making	• Change in peer group (depending on circumstances) • Independence from parents/carers • Patterns of behaviour around drug taking/ alcohol and sexual behaviour more apparent and established • Recognition and acceptance into 'adult' world • Established relationships • Expectation that decisions are the responsibility of the young person • Need/desire to leave home • Parents/carers have much less significant role/influence	• Significant decisions about future transitions will be taken • New learning and training opportunities • Greater financial freedom/less financial freedom • Move away from home • Managing budgets • Applying for jobs/university/training • Preparing for interviews

siblings, abusive relationships and cultural differences have not been identified here. These factors exist, will be shared by many young people and may well be raised in discussions in PLD sessions, but for the most part they do not provide the kind of broad themes or areas of concern that are likely to be common to most young people.

So, if the youth support worker is faced with a particular group of young people, how do they decide what should form the focus for the PLD sessions that they will be facilitating? The case studies set out below provide examples from a range of youth support professionals who have been asked by the institution in which they work, or have decided as part of their professional role, to facilitate PLD group work. When reading the case studies, it is helpful to identify and reflect on the perceived needs of each group.

Question

What would you consider to be an appropriate focus for PLD sessions in each case?

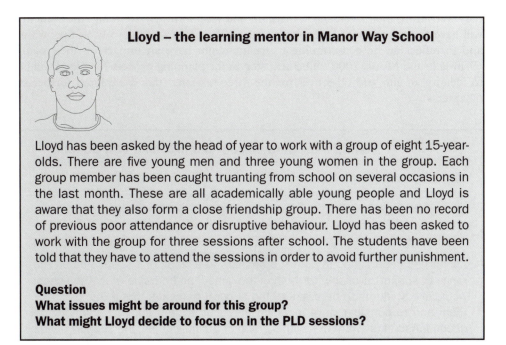

Lloyd – the learning mentor in Manor Way School

Lloyd has been asked by the head of year to work with a group of eight 15-year-olds. There are five young men and three young women in the group. Each group member has been caught truanting from school on several occasions in the last month. These are all academically able young people and Lloyd is aware that they also form a close friendship group. There has been no record of previous poor attendance or disruptive behaviour. Lloyd has been asked to work with the group for three sessions after school. The students have been told that they have to attend the sessions in order to avoid further punishment.

Question
What issues might be around for this group?
What might Lloyd decide to focus on in the PLD sessions?

In the case above, Lloyd will consider what might be the underlying reasons for the truancy to have taken place. He knows that the group is made up of able students who are expected to do well in their exams and he is also aware that there are no general concerns about other aspects of each individual's behaviour. There may be a number of reasons for truancy:

1   Peer pressure might play a part with one or two dominant group members taking the lead.

2   Boredom may be a factor with the group feeling that lessons in school are not stimulating or challenging enough.

3   Group members may be feeling stressed by their fast-approaching examinations and may be 'running away' from the pressure.

4   The group is struggling to find an identity and rebel from the label of 'good' and 'able' students by pushing the boundaries and taking risks.

Lloyd is aware that any of these factors could play a part in recent events (and there may be others too). He decides that the PLD sessions should provide a forum in which these issues can be explored, but he does not feel that making the focus or topic of the session 'Truancy' will help to engage the group. He is also clear that the young people concerned are likely to view the sessions with him as a 'punishment' for their truancy. He is keen that this should not be the case, and that each young person should have the opportunity to gain positive outcomes from the sessions. Lloyd decides to concentrate the focus of the sessions on a future-oriented scenario, whereby the group members will have an opportunity to reflect on what they want from their lives, short, medium and long term. By so doing, the students will have the opportunity to think about how they plan to achieve what they want, and to reflect on how continuing to truant might have an impact on their plans (Winslade and Monk, 2000). The next step in the planning process for Lloyd will be to identify an aim and objectives for the three sessions (this is explored further in Chapter 4).

Ashraf – the personal adviser in Manor Way School

Ashraf has been asked to deliver a session to a class of 13-year-olds on the range of support available to them in the school and outside of it. The school would like students to be aware of the support networks that are in place for them and to consider ways in which they can access support should it be needed. Ashraf is aware that with a group of 30 individuals, the support needs could be numerous and varied. However, he is also clear that there are likely to be issues requiring support that are common to many 13-year-olds.

Question
What issues might be around for the group?
What might Ashraf decide to focus on in the PLD session?

Assessing the needs of individuals in a large group such as this can be difficult. However, Ashraf is aware of certain key factors that will be common to most young people in this class of 13-year-olds:

1   They are making choices about school subjects.
2   They will be under increased pressure to 'do well' and gain qualifications.
3   They are reaching adolescence and puberty.
4   They are developing an identity.
5   They may be wanting to experiment with drugs, alcohol, relationships and sex.
6   They may be experiencing conflict with their parents/carers.

So, in this PLD session, Ashraf plans to help the group to reflect on what their support needs might be during the course of the next few years. In addition, he will enable them to consider strategies for meeting these needs and will provide them with information about who and what might be available to offer support in a range of areas. Like Lloyd, Ashraf is not yet at the point where the session is planned in any detail. He is simply beginning the process by establishing a focus.

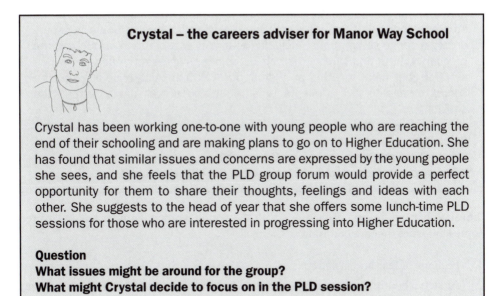

Crystal – the careers adviser for Manor Way School

Crystal has been working one-to-one with young people who are reaching the end of their schooling and are making plans to go on to Higher Education. She has found that similar issues and concerns are expressed by the young people she sees, and she feels that the PLD group forum would provide a perfect opportunity for them to share their thoughts, feelings and ideas with each other. She suggests to the head of year that she offers some lunch-time PLD sessions for those who are interested in progressing into Higher Education.

Question
What issues might be around for the group?
What might Crystal decide to focus on in the PLD session?

Crystal has made a note of the key issues that arise frequently in one-to-one discussions about Higher Education with young people. They are as follows:

1   How to decide on the right course of study.
2   Where might be the best place to study?
3   Moving away from home.

4   Managing finances and budgeting.

5   Whether or not to take a 'year out' before going into Higher Education.

Crystal decides to offer three PLD sessions. The first will focus on decision making concerning both the course of study and the place of study; the second will explore issues surrounding living away from home; and the third will investigate the possibility of taking a 'year out'. The sessions will be optional whereby young people will choose whether they attend one, two or all three, depending on their individual situation. Having decided on a broad focus, Crystal is now ready to begin the next step in the planning process.

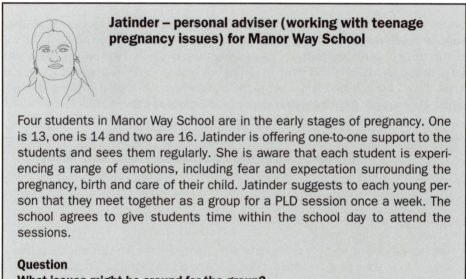

Jatinder – personal adviser (working with teenage pregnancy issues) for Manor Way School

Four students in Manor Way School are in the early stages of pregnancy. One is 13, one is 14 and two are 16. Jatinder is offering one-to-one support to the students and sees them regularly. She is aware that each student is experiencing a range of emotions, including fear and expectation surrounding the pregnancy, birth and care of their child. Jatinder suggests to each young person that they meet together as a group for a PLD session once a week. The school agrees to give students time within the school day to attend the sessions.

Question
What issues might be around for the group?
What might Jatinder decide to focus on in the PLD sessions?

Through her one-to-one discussions with the young women, Jatinder has uncovered some key issues that are common to them all:

1   Feelings of fear and isolation.

2   Anxiety about the pregnancy and birth – how can they stay healthy, how will they cope?

3   Financial concerns – how will they provide for the baby?

4   Support – who will be there to help a young parent?

5   The future – what might the future hold in relation to their education, training or employment opportunities?

Jatinder decides to structure four PLD sessions initially, but she is flexible about this, and is prepared to continue to work with the group as other issues emerge. She is keen that students have the opportunity to offer support to each other through their shared experience, but she also feels that the sessions should remain purposeful. Jatinder plans that session one will focus on staying healthy through the pregnancy and birth, thus providing the young women with the opportunity to share their fears and anxieties about this. In session two, the group will concentrate on financial planning and budgeting for when the baby arrives. The third session will examine the support that is available following the birth and will identify how this can be accessed. Finally, the fourth session will offer an exploration of 'the future' and what this might look like, including a discussion of each student's hopes and fears. Although Jatinder now has an idea of focus for each session, she has not yet taken the planning process further.

Sam – the youth worker employed by the local youth service

As mentioned in Chapter 1, Sam works with groups of young people (and sometimes their families) as part of an extended schools project where students and their families are invited to use the facilities of the school, outside teaching hours, to enhance their development. Sam is aware that a group of young men aged between 14 and 16 are often kicking a ball around outside the school or sitting on the school wall, but do not take part in any of the activities available. Often the young men's behaviour is disruptive. They shout at passers-by and use intimidating language and gestures. Sam considers approaching the young men to suggest working together as a group.

Question
What issues might be around for the group?
What might Sam decide to focus on in PLD sessions?

Having observed the group, Sam has noticed a number of key underlying issues. He senses that individuals are:

1   bored and lacking in motivation;
2   finding a common identity that is focused on disruptive and aggressive behaviour;
3   being influenced by dominant young men in the group and 'going along' with what is expected for fear of being ridiculed;
4   lacking in confidence and self-esteem;
5   able to 'tap into' their energy sources and have creative ideas, even if these often result in negative behaviours.

Sam wants to offer an alternative to the young men that will appeal to them, but will also provide more than simply a diversionary tactic to keep them off the streets. He decides to approach the group, but he is aware that they may be defensive and hostile to his overtures. He plans to suggest the possibility of involving the young men as 'coaches', working with an after-school football project with younger pupils. However, in order to be accepted as coaches, they will need to undergo what Sam describes as 'training', but will actually be PLD sessions. These sessions will provide the young men with the opportunity to build their self-esteem and confidence through discussions and activities, as well as introducing them to football coaching techniques. Now that Sam has decided on a focus for the PLD sessions, he will need to begin the planning of each session in more detail.

In each of the five case studies outlined above, the youth support worker has taken time to consider the needs of the individuals in the group at this point in their lives. The worker has assessed the ways in which PLD sessions may play a part in addressing these needs. So far, no specific planning has taken place, no aims have been set, no activities have been structured and the groups have not yet met together. However, the youth support worker has taken the first step in the planning and preparation of the PLD sessions.

Clearly, there is a danger in selecting a focus for the PLD session that does not meet the needs of the group. For example, if Sam, in our last case study, had decided that the focus of PLD group work for this group of disengaged 14- to 16-year-old young men should be on 'preparing for higher education', it is unlikely that the members of the group would 'buy in' to the sessions. That is not to say that at some future point, members of this group would not benefit from such a session, but at this time it does not meet their needs in any way. So, if the focus for the session does not meet the perceived needs of the group, what might happen? The list set out below summarizes the possible consequences of facilitating PLD sessions without first having undertaken an assessment of needs within the group:

- Group members become restless and fidgety.
- Group members appear lethargic and apathetic.
- Group members feel disengaged.
- Group members refuse to participate and cooperate.
- Group members become aggressive or disruptive.
- The relationship between group members and the youth support worker is affected adversely.
- Group members decide not to attend further PLD sessions.
- No positive outcomes are achieved.

When the needs of the group have been established and an assessment of the issues that young people face at certain points in their lives has been made, youth support workers, like Lloyd, Ashraf, Jatinder, Crystal and Sam, can move on and consider a range of topics that might be worked on in PLD sessions. Only once this assessment has taken place can youth support workers feel confident that the topics they select for their PLD sessions will be relevant to the young people with whom they work.

Choosing a topic

The case studies above demonstrate clearly the relationship between assessing needs and identifying a topic. In each case, in very general terms, ideas for possible topics have been considered. Of course, as yet there is no 'fine detail' concerning what the sessions will contain, but there is a clear focus to the sessions that youth support workers have the opportunity to build on in their planning. If PLD group work is to do as its title suggests and address the personal learning and development needs of young people, then it is these personal and developmental needs that will form the focus of each session. Building on the range of needs that were identified in the diagram in Figure 3.1 earlier in this chapter, Table 3.2 proposes some possible 'topics' that may relate to the developmental, social and educational needs of young people.

Table 3.2 suggests just a few ideas for topics for PLD group sessions under the headings of physical/emotional, social and education/transition. Of course, youth support professionals operate in a range of contexts and they will identify many more PLD topics that are relevant to the young people with whom they work. Readers will notice that 'overcoming barriers' resides in each column; this should act as a timely reminder that the work of youth support practitioners, regardless of their specific job

Table 3.2 Topics for PLD group sessions

Topics to address physical/ emotional factors	Topics to address social factors	Topics to address educational/transition factors
• Self-awareness • Keeping healthy • Sexual health • Diet and nutrition • Bereavement or family breakdown • Managing pregnancy • Parenting skills • Dealing with stress • Managing change • Raising self-esteem and confidence building • Dealing with and reporting abuse • Anger management • Overcoming barriers	• Bullying • Assertiveness • Relationship building • Peer group pressure • Stereotyping • Staying safe • Drugs/alcohol awareness • Time management • Behaviour management • Negotiation skills • Communication skills • Planning leisure time • Managing conflict • Problem-solving • Team building • Developing an identity • Overcoming barriers	• Options at 13, 16, 18 • Decision making • Moving on to higher education • Career opportunities • Job applications • CV writing • Interview skills • Study skills • Work experience • The world of work • Developing transferable skills • Overcoming barriers

title, is concerned primarily with helping young people to overcome the barriers that they face in their lives. These barriers may be emotional, physical, social or concerned with learning, education and transitions within and following, statutory schooling. Whatever the barrier for any individual, it is likely that a number of other young people find themselves faced with similar circumstances or issues. Therefore, PLD group work provides a forum in which young people can examine the barriers, share their concerns and experiences and, ultimately find ways to overcome, or at least reduce, their own barriers to progression.

Summary

This chapter set out to consider the first steps in planning PLD sessions. The FAAST model is introduced, which provides youth support workers with a helpful starting point for planning their PLD group sessions. It stresses the significance of beginning the planning process by identifying a *focus* for the session, which will meet the needs of the young people who are participating. In order to establish a *focus*, the youth support worker should first reflect on the perceived needs of the group. In many cases, PLD sessions will be planned as a result of youth support workers identifying common issues or needs among individual young people with whom they are already working. They will know the young people and will have recognized the shared areas of need. This was evident in the case studies featuring Jatinder and Crystal. However, there may be times when the youth support worker has not had direct contact with the young people themselves. In cases such as these, the youth support practitioner must make an assessment of the group at this point in their development, and then decide on a relevant topic that will address their perceived needs. The case studies featuring Lloyd and Ashraf demonstrate this scenario. Where the young people are not directly known to the youth support worker, practitioners will need to draw on their knowledge of shared emotional, physical, social and educational developmental factors in order to inform their choice of topic.

As stated at the start of this chapter, subsequent chapters investigate each stage of the FAAST model in turn. However, the importance of step one, identifying a focus, should not be understated. The youth support worker who has not assessed the needs of the group and, consequently, constructs a session based on a range of ill-informed assumptions and disconnected activities is at risk of delivering a negative experience for young people that has little or nothing in the way of positive outcomes for the participants.

Questions

The following questions and suggested activity will assist reflection on the key themes addressed in this chapter.

1 **How does the 'F' of the FAAST model inform the planning of PLD group work?**

2 **What are the key issues that young people face in their development?**

3 **What should the youth support worker do in order to select an appropriate topic for a PLD session?**

4 **How might PLD sessions help young people to overcome barriers that they face?**

Activity

Consider the young people in your own work context with whom you are working individually, but not in groups. Reflect on their needs and identify common areas. From this assessment, list some possible topics that might form the focus for PLD group work sessions.

4

Setting aims and objectives leading to positive outcomes

Learning Objectives

- Define the notion of a session 'aim'
- Clarify the importance of setting an aim
- Describe the concept of a session objective
- Assess the significance of setting objectives
- Identify the link between aims, objectives and outcomes

Introduction

Once an appropriate topic for PLD sessions has been identified (with thought given to its applicability to the needs of the target group), the next step in the planning process is to set an aim for the session and to identify appropriate session objectives that should lead to positive outcomes for the participants (Reynolds, 1994; Malekoff, 2004; Doel, 2006). This chapter focuses on these specific aspects of the planning process. It continues to utilize the FAAST model, introduced in Chapter 3, which provides youth support workers with a suggested chronology for planning, preparing and delivering PLD sessions:

- Focus
- Aim
- Activities
- Structure
- Techniques

So far, we have established the importance of identifying a Focus for PLD sessions, ensuring that the needs of *individual* group members are being addressed, albeit in a *group* context. This chapter continues to follow the FAAST model by examining the means by which a session aim and associated objectives are determined. The case study examples introduced in Chapter 3 are developed more fully, providing the opportunity to follow the planning process through in detail.

Before moving on to explore in detail how the session aim and objectives are set, it is important to reach an understanding about the terminology used and to be clear about how aims, objectives and outcomes each fulfil a separate but related function. This is particularly important given the use of a range of terms applied to the setting of aims and objectives that essentially describes the same process. Geldard and Geldard make the point succinctly that:

> It is essential for leaders to set clear goals for each session so the group does not deteriorate into a purposeless group and so that outcomes can be evaluated with regard to these goals.
>
> (Geldard and Geldard, 2001: 68)

The terminology used here specifies 'goals' and 'outcomes'. This is appropriate, but begs the question how do 'goals' and 'objectives' differ and what is meant by the 'outcome?' The chapter begins then by clarifying the language used and identifying the key features of the aim, objectives and outcomes. It goes on to examine how these concepts are applied in practice and it works through the planning process with Lloyd, Ashraf, Crystal, Jatinder and Sam, as they consider the aim and objectives for the PLD sessions that they were planning in Chapter 3.

Making sense of the language

For PLD sessions to be purposeful, relevant and structured, it is important that they have a stated aim and specific objectives that work towards positive outcomes. In order for youth support workers to set an aim, establish objectives and identify desired outcomes, they need to know what each term means and what the function is in the context of PLD group work. In the same way that planning group sessions follows a chronology (the FAAST model), the determining of an aim, objectives and outcomes should also be undertaken in order, with the aim informing the objectives and the objectives establishing the session content, which will lead to the outcomes. It makes sense, therefore, to 'unpick' the terminology by focusing on the first concept, the session aim.

The aim

A dictionary definition of 'aim' suggests 'a purpose or intention; a desired outcome' (1998). In group work terms this means setting out clearly *what* will be achieved in the session, but not identifying specifically *how* it will be achieved. In most cases PLD sessions will have *one* overall aim, not several. Put simply, the aim of a session describes its purpose. It establishes the focus for the group work and also signposts the direction that the session will take. For example, a youth support worker might be planning a session where the broad topic identified is 'self-awareness'. A number of possible aims for group work on self-awareness could be appropriate. Each would depend on the specific emphasis and direction that the youth support worker has decided would be most relevant for the particular individual group members. The list below suggests some possible aims for a self-awareness PLD session:

- Describe my strengths and identify areas I want to develop.
- Identify the effects of my behaviour on others.
- Recognize my skills and abilities.
- Develop strategies for managing my anger.
- Explore what I want from my future.

Each of the session aims outlined above relates to the general topic of self-awareness, and yet each suggests a quite different focus for the PLD session. It could be argued that the topic of self-awareness is broad in its scope and therefore it is not surprising that a whole host of possible session aims can be identified. However, even in the case of a topic such as sexual health, where the focus is less far ranging, the aim identified for the session will dictate its direction. For example:

- How to keep safe in sexual relationships.
- How to deal with the effects of peer pressure in relation to sex.
- Where to find help and who to go to for support with an unplanned pregnancy.

In each of the examples outlined, the general topic title remains the same (self-awareness or sexual health) but the aim identified for each session sets out the focus and to some extent, although not in any detail, the content of the session. To illustrate this further, we can return to the five group sessions identified in Chapter 3 with Lloyd, Ashraf, Crystal, Jatinder and Sam. Each of these youth support workers has assessed the needs of their group and identified an appropriate topic (or focus) to address in PLD group work. The next step is to select an aim for each of their planned sessions.

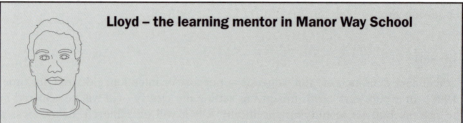

Lloyd – the learning mentor in Manor Way School

Lloyd has been asked to work with a group of eight 15-year-olds who have been truanting from school. He has assessed the needs of the group in order to identify a focus for the three sessions he will be facilitating with them. He has decided to structure each session around a future-oriented scenario in order to engage the young people and help them to explore how their current attitudes and behaviour may have an impact on their future lives. He has selected an appropriate topic and is using a 'working title' for his own planning purposes for each of the three sessions:

1 What I want from my life in the short term.
2 Medium-term planning.
3 Longer-term goals.

Lloyd must now begin to translate his working title for each session into a clearly stated aim.

Question
What aim could he select that suggests a focus, purpose and direction for each session?

Lloyd has a range of options from which to choose. He knows that setting the aim will play a significant part in establishing the tone and direction and will, most importantly, specify the personal learning and development of the group members. He is keen to ensure that although the PLD sessions have, in part, been organized as a punitive measure for their truancy, the group members are encouraged to engage with the content and to achieve something meaningful as a result of attending. He identifies three possible aims for each session from which he will select one:

Session One: What I want from my life in the short term (working title).

Possible aims are:

1   to design my own life plan for the next year;
2   to identify strategies for overcoming barriers to achieving my personal, social and educational goals in the next year;
3   how to organize my life: setting priorities for the next year.

Session Two: Medium-term planning (working title).

Possible aims are:

1   to identify and assess options at the end of statutory education;
2   to consider my life priorities after 16;
3   how to organize my life: my future after school has ended.

Session Three: Longer-term goals (working title).

Possible aims are:

1   to identify my preferred long-term career options;
2   to consider my life priorities in the future;
3   how to organize my life: my long-term life goals.

Lloyd decides to select the third aim in each list. His decision is influenced by the following:

- The aim he has selected in each case provides a title for the session that is easily understood and will engage the group members, encouraging them to take ownership for decision making about their future.
- Often young people are anxious about the future and their transition into an adult world. Lloyd thinks that this anxiety may have had a negative impact on individual behaviour. The aim he has set for each session will support the young people in thinking about what the future might hold in a safe and contained environment.
- Using the words 'how to organize' in each case suggests an active and purposeful session, whereby the young people will take ownership of their planning.
- There is a clear link between each of the sessions that demonstrates progression.

Having decided on an aim for each session, the next step for Lloyd is to consider objectives that link to the aim. This is examined later in the chapter, but first, we will return to the other youth support workers engaged in planning PLD sessions.

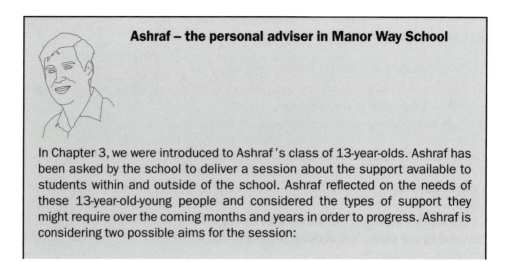

Ashraf – the personal adviser in Manor Way School

In Chapter 3, we were introduced to Ashraf's class of 13-year-olds. Ashraf has been asked by the school to deliver a session about the support available to students within and outside of the school. Ashraf reflected on the needs of these 13-year-old-young people and considered the types of support they might require over the coming months and years in order to progress. Ashraf is considering two possible aims for the session:

1 What support I need to help me succeed at school.
2 Who I can go to when I need help.

Question
Which of these two aims do you think Ashraf should choose, and why?

Either aim would be quite acceptable, clearly linked to the generic topic of the PLD session. However, Ashraf decides to select the second of the two possible aims for his session. He has assessed the needs of the group and is aware that at 13 years of age, there are a number of factors that will have an impact on young peoples' lives, as discussed in detail in Chapter 3. He decides that the second of the two possible aims broadens the session and enables the students to focus, not just on the support available in school, but also on the individuals and agencies that can offer help in all aspects of their lives.

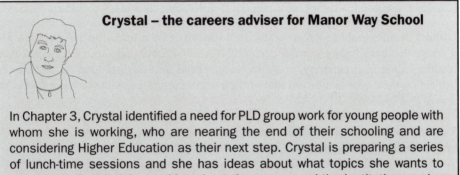

Crystal – the careers adviser for Manor Way School

In Chapter 3, Crystal identified a need for PLD group work for young people with whom she is working, who are nearing the end of their schooling and are considering Higher Education as their next step. Crystal is preparing a series of lunch-time sessions and she has ideas about what topics she wants to cover, including decision making about the course and the institution, coping with moving away from home, managing budgets and taking a 'year out'. Crystal has identified two possible aims for the first session that will focus on choosing a course of study. These are:

1 What to study: how to make a decision about my preferred subject.
2 The impact my subject choice might have on future decisions about my life.

Question
Which of these two aims do you think Crystal should choose and why?

Again, like Ashraf, either aim is perfectly acceptable, but Crystal reflects that the pupils she has spoken to during one-to-one interactions have consistently expressed worries about the impact of their choice of Higher Education course on their future life and career plans. She decides, therefore, that the second aim will address these anxieties most directly.

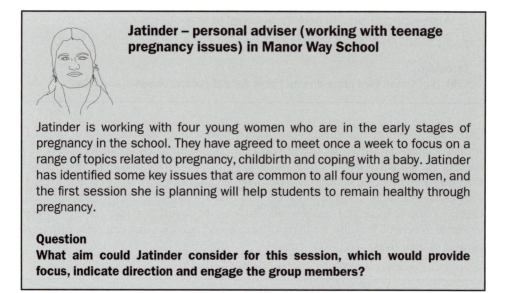

Jatinder – personal adviser (working with teenage pregnancy issues) in Manor Way School

Jatinder is working with four young women who are in the early stages of pregnancy in the school. They have agreed to meet once a week to focus on a range of topics related to pregnancy, childbirth and coping with a baby. Jatinder has identified some key issues that are common to all four young women, and the first session she is planning will help students to remain healthy through pregnancy.

Question
What aim could Jatinder consider for this session, which would provide focus, indicate direction and engage the group members?

Jatinder decides that she will focus the first session on healthy eating and exercise. She is aware that each young woman currently has little knowledge about what constitutes healthy eating in pregnancy, and she is concerned that this may have a detrimental impact on their own health and that of their unborn children. She therefore makes the aim of this session:

Keeping healthy: What I should eat and how I should exercise during pregnancy to keep me and my baby healthy?

Sam – the youth worker employed by the local youth service

Sam has decided to plan a series of sessions for a group of 14- to 16-year-old young men, who exhibit disruptive and negative behaviour outside the school gates during the early evening when a range of after-school activities are on offer. Sam plans to include the young men by asking them to be involved in providing football coaching to younger students as part of a structured pro-gramme of activities. However, initially he needs to engage the young men and help to build their confidence and self-esteem. Sam plans his first session to focus on raising self-esteem. He needs to decide on a specific aim.

Question
If you were to plan this session, what aim would you set?

Unlike the other case study examples Sam has *not* selected the aim for this session. You have been given the opportunity to decide the aim for this session on raising self-esteem, and you will be given a further opportunity later in this chapter to work with your aim to set appropriate objectives for the session, thus following through the planning process yourself.

Activity

It might be helpful to write your suggested aim down, so that you are able to return to it later in this chapter.

There should, by now, be clarity about what the aim is and why it is important to set one for every PLD session. It can be helpful to think of the aim as the 'overarching title' or purpose of the session, which introduces the topic to be addressed and clarifies a particular focus. Without a stated aim, the PLD session is likely to be purposeless and lack direction. It runs the risk of, at best, achieving very little, and, at worst, having a negative impact on the students involved.

Now that the concept of the aim is clearly established, it is important to consider the purpose of the objectives. What is an objective, how does it connect to the aim and what impact will it have on the planning of the session?

The objective

'The objectives define what participants will learn' (Payne, 2005: 136). This statement sets out clearly and succinctly how the session objectives relate to, but are different from, the session aim. Where the aim provides an overall title for the session, stating the topic to be addressed and suggesting a purpose and sense of direction, the objective does something different. The objective (or objectives, as there are likely to be more than one for each session) clarifies in precise terms what it is that each young person will have the opportunity to achieve during the PLD session. The objective should be clear and specific, and, most importantly, both achievable in the session and verifiable at its end. By setting objectives at the outset, the youth support worker can be confident that the group work will be focused and purposeful.

Alongside establishing the aim, setting objectives forms the other critical aspect of the planning stage of PLD sessions, and it is often the part that is missing or rushed when youth support workers are engaging with the planning process. This could be for a number of reasons, including uncertainty about what an objective is, lack of regard to its significance, and excitement about discovering an interesting activity to undertake in the session. But by setting out in precise terms what participants will have the opportunity to achieve, the youth support worker is providing a firm foundation on which the fine detail of the session can be built. A simply applied tool can be used when setting objectives. It is summarized by the acronym 'PHOTO', which stands for **P**articipants **H**ave the **O**pportunity **TO** . . . When considering what objectives to set, youth support workers can use PHOTO as a pre-fix, thus ensuring that the objectives are active, meaningful and inform the session content.

To go back to an earlier example in this chapter of a PLD session on self-awareness where the aim is, 'Developing strengths and identifying weaknesses', a number of possible objectives might be identified. For example:

Participants Have the Opportunity To (PHOTO) . . .

- list three things they do well;
- identify three things about themselves that they would like to develop;
- discuss strategies for improving the areas they have identified;
- describe three action points to help them improve the areas they have identified.

Each of the objectives listed above is specific, achievable within a PLD session and can be evaluated at the end of the session. To ensure that each objective can be evaluated, it is important that the language used is verifiable. For instance, in the examples above, the verb used in each case (i.e. list, identify, discuss, describe) is verifiable (i.e. an observer would be able to identify that these things happened in the session). The youth support worker knows that the participants have had the opportunity within the session to list, identify, discuss and describe. Indeed, in the next step of the planning process, the practitioner will ensure that the activities within the session will enable this to happen (exploring the relationship between session objectives and appropriate activities is discussed more fully in Chapter 5). But if the youth support worker chooses unspecific language that cannot be verified when setting objectives, the evaluation of the session will be less effective. Figure 4.1 sets out words to choose from and words to avoid when setting objectives. The left-hand column selects words that are verbs; 'doing' words that can be verified and 'evidenced' at the end of the session. Law (2001) emphasizes the use of verbs as being critical to the learning process because they do not simply state what should be learned, but how learning takes place. The right-hand column, by contrast, can only be measured if observed over time or assessed in some way.

Words to use		Words to avoid	
List	Set out	Consider	Enable
Write	Observe	Understand	Appreciate
Describe	Tell	Think about	Be aware of
Draw	Select	Develop	Review
Construct	Decide	Explore	Revise
Identify	Evaluate	Examine	Discover

Figure 4.1 Words to use and words to avoid when setting objectives

> **Question**
>
> Think about your own planning of PLD sessions. How effectively do you choose specific and verifiable language to express what you want participants to achieve in their PLD sessions?

Now that there is more clarity about what objectives look like and why they are important, we can return to the five sessions for which the 'aim' has been set earlier in the chapter. Lloyd, Ashraf, Crystal, Jatinder and Sam have identified the aim for their sessions and are now ready to set the objectives for each. Before we return to the case studies, it is important to be aware of one more thing when setting objectives. The youth support worker should be clear about how long the PLD session will last. The number of objectives set for a 30-minute session will differ considerably to the number set for a whole-day workshop. Youth support workers need to be realistic about what can be achieved in the time they have available. If they identify too many objectives, the session is likely to feel rushed and is in danger of not achieving its goals. If too few objectives are set, the session risks 'running out of steam', and the young people are likely to become disengaged. As a simple guide, a 45-minute PLD session could, normally, accommodate two to four objectives.

> **Questions**
>
> In the examples below, how effectively do you think that the session objectives have been set?
>
> Do they conform to the guidelines established in this chapter? Can PHOTO be inserted before each objective?
>
> Is the language used specific and verifiable?
>
> Is the number of objectives set realistic in the time available?

Lloyd – the learning mentor in Manor Way School

Session one – AIM: How to organize my life; setting priorities for the next year

Lloyd is working with a group of eight 15-year-olds. He is planning a series of three PLD sessions. Each session will last for 45 minutes. He has set the aim for all three sessions and he is now ready to identify appropriate objectives that link to the aim, but give clear direction about what each young person will have the opportunity to achieve in the session (PHOTO). He begins with Session one. Lloyd decides that realistically, in a 45-minute session, the group is likely to achieve three or four objectives.

Question
What objectives might you consider setting for Session one?

In order to set the objectives for the session, Lloyd uses the PHOTO acronym as a starting point. He then selects the following objectives, using words that are specific and verifiable.

Participants have the opportunity to:

- describe three things in their school life they enjoy and feel good about, and three goals in relation to education that they would like to achieve in the next year;
- list the barriers to achieving their goals;
- identify strategies for overcoming the barriers to achieve their goals;
- write an individual action plan for the next month.

Lloyd is clear that each of the objectives listed relates to the overall aim of the session. He is also confident that the objectives are specific and measurable. The only doubt he has is how realistic it will be to achieve all four objectives in a 45-minute session. He decides that he can be flexible about the final objective (writing an individual action plan), as he will be seeing the group again for two more PLD sessions. He may wait until the final session in the series of three to give participants the opportunity to decide on an action plan for their future development. He can now begin to assess a range of activities that will ensure that the objectives for the session will be met. We will return to Lloyd in Chapter 5 to see how his planning is progressing.

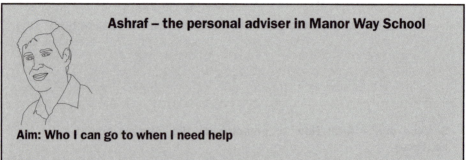

Ashraf – the personal adviser in Manor Way School

Aim: Who I can go to when I need help

Ashraf has set the aim for his session with a class of 13-year-olds in the school. He has been allocated a one-hour slot in which to introduce the students to the range of support that is available to them both within and outside the school. Ashraf sets the following objectives for the session.

Participants have the opportunity to:

- think about the support that might be needed in relation to education, social and personal development;
- consider individuals and agencies who can offer support;
- know how to recognize that you need support;
- be aware of how to access the support that is available.

Question
How effectively do these objectives adhere to best practice in setting objectives?
How might you write them differently?

Ashraf talks his ideas through with a more experienced youth support worker who makes the point that the objectives, although linked to the session aim, and addressing the needs of the group members, cannot be verified. As a result, where Ashraf has written 'think about', he amends this to 'describe', he changes 'consider' to 'list', he revises 'know' and writes 'identify' and finally he alters 'be aware of' to 'set out'. He is now confident that at the end of the session, he will be able to evaluate clearly how far the objectives have been addressed. He is also well placed to continue his planning by identifying activities that will enable the objectives to be met.

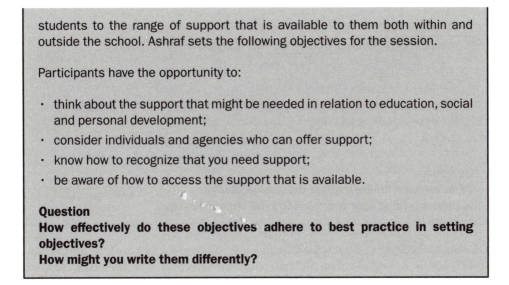

Crystal – the careers adviser for Manor Way School

Aim: The impact my subject choice might have on future decisions about my life

Crystal has established the aim for her first lunch-time session with young people who are considering moving on from school to Higher Education. She has identified anxiety in many of the students about choosing appropriate courses. In particular, they are concerned about how this decision may have an impact on future career ideas. Thus, the aim addresses this aspect of the decision-making process. Crystal sets the following objectives whereby participants have the opportunity to:

- set out subject areas in broad categories (e.g. technical, scientific);

- identify a range of 'job families' (e.g. medical, caring, literary);
- make links between the broad subject areas and job families;
- list their own preferred subject area;
- select their own preferred job family;
- describe any job families where they may experience barriers if they choose their preferred subject area;
- write down three action steps to take to research their ideas further.

Question
What are your feelings about these objectives?
Is there anything that you think Crystal should change?

On reflection, Crystal decides that although she will have the whole of the lunch hour, realistically it is unlikely that the full range of objectives will be met within the time constraints. The students will be engaging with the session while eating their lunch and therefore Crystal knows that activities will inevitably take longer and fewer objectives are likely to be met. She revises her list by deciding that the first three objectives are not necessary. Rather than focus on the 'general', she decides that it will be of more use to encourage the students to reflect on the specifics of their own situations. The agreed objectives are therefore that participants have the opportunity to:

- list their own preferred subject area;
- select their own preferred job family;
- describe any job families where they may experience barriers if they choose their preferred subject area;
- write down three action steps to take to research their ideas further.

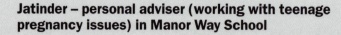

Jatinder – personal adviser (working with teenage pregnancy issues) in Manor Way School

Aim: Keeping healthy; what I should eat and how I should exercise during pregnancy to keep me and my baby healthy

Jatinder has decided on the aim for her first session with the four young women in the school who are pregnant, but has not given any thought to setting objectives. She is unaware of the importance of this aspect of the planning process.

Question

What are the potential risks for the PLD session if Jatinder does not set any objectives?

Jatinder discusses the session with her colleague Kelly, a teaching assistant in the school. Kelly raises the issue of the lack of objectives. Jatinder replies that she simply does not have time to set aside for more detailed planning. We see the consequences of this in Chapter 5 when Jatinder sets about choosing appropriate activities for the session.

Sam – the youth worker employed by the local youth service

You will remember that Sam is preparing a session on 'raising self-esteem' for a group of 14- to 16-year-old young men. The session will last for one hour and you have already helped Sam in his planning by deciding on an appropriate aim for the session.

Activity

You are now going to assist Sam further by setting three or four objectives that link to the aim. Go back to the aim that you identified for the session and use the guidelines set out in this chapter as a starting point (i.e. PHOTO and use concrete, specific and verifiable language).

So far, the concept of setting the aim for a session and clarifying the relationship between the aim and the objectives has been examined. Finally, the chapter establishes how the aim and objectives set for the group work lead to *outcomes* for the young people following the session.

The outcome

For a PLD session to be truly effective, it must be part of an ongoing process of personal learning and development. Therefore, any PLD session will set out to enhance that process, and provide young people with key skills, abilities and tools to enable them to apply their learning in their lives. This application of learning and the subsequent changes it makes to the life of each young person is described as 'the outcome'. Unlike the objectives, which can be evaluated at the end of each PLD session, the outcome for each individual will not be known until after the session, when participants have the opportunity to reflect on their learning and apply it to any decisions they make, and subsequent actions they take (this links clearly to the concept of experiential learning discussed in Chapter 2). While the objectives for the session are the same for each participant, the outcome is likely to differ. How each young person applies their learning will be based on their individual situation. The outcomes for participant A may not be the same as the outcomes for participant B even though they have attended the same session, with the same aim and the same objectives.

Law (2001) informs our thinking about 'outcomes' with his DOTS analysis that describes learning outcomes in relation to key areas of personal learning and development. DOTS stands for:

- **D**ecision making
- **O**pportunity awareness
- **T**ransition skills
- **S**elf-awareness

This model is examined in more detail in Chapter 10.

Returning to Lloyd's session, which now has an aim and objectives, we can consider a range of possible outcomes for group members.

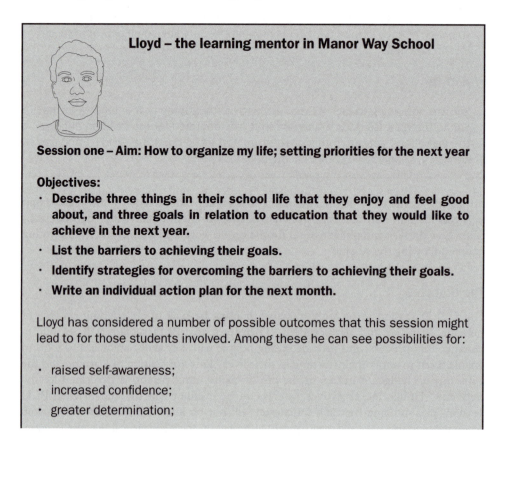

Lloyd – the learning mentor in Manor Way School

Session one – Aim: How to organize my life; setting priorities for the next year

Objectives:
- **Describe three things in their school life that they enjoy and feel good about, and three goals in relation to education that they would like to achieve in the next year.**
- **List the barriers to achieving their goals.**
- **Identify strategies for overcoming the barriers to achieving their goals.**
- **Write an individual action plan for the next month.**

Lloyd has considered a number of possible outcomes that this session might lead to for those students involved. Among these he can see possibilities for:

- raised self-awareness;
- increased confidence;
- greater determination;

- application of practical strategies – planning action steps;
- strengthened commitment to education and development;
- increase in decision-making skills.

Although Lloyd thinks that any of the outcomes listed above are possible, he has no way of measuring them directly following the session. Lloyd will need to wait and see how effective his PLD session has been, as the young people who have taken part draw on their learning from the session and put it into practice in their day-to-day lives.

Reflecting back on the sessions that are being prepared by other youth support workers in this chapter, it is possible to identify a range of possible positive outcomes for each, which would be far too long to list here. A possible exception to this is Jatinder's session, which does not, at present, have any set objectives and is therefore likely to lack direction and purpose. In this case, the outcomes for the young people involved are at risk.

Summary

This chapter set out to clarify the meaning of the terms 'aim', 'objectives' and 'outcomes' and to consider how each applies to PLD group work. The terms themselves have different meanings and separate functions; however, the link between them is clear. The *aim* introduces the session topic. It provides a title for the session that establishes a clear focus, sense of purpose and direction relating to the topic. The *objectives* link to the aim, but go further in providing guidance as to what will actually take place in the session. The objectives offer a concrete, specific and verifiable set of tasks that participants will undertake (PHOTO), and, if effective will lead to positive outcomes. The *outcomes* will only be realized following the session where participants have the opportunity to apply their learning to their lives.

As stated earlier, this important aspect of the planning process is often hurried, or in some cases missed out altogether. Where this happens the young people who are participating in the session may be unclear about what they are doing and why they are doing it. Youth support workers may find themselves asking similar questions as the session progresses.

Questions

The following questions and suggested activity will assist reflection on the key themes addressed in this chapter:

1 **What is the link between the aim, the objectives and the outcomes of a PLD session?**

2 **Why is it important to use specific and concrete language when setting objectives?**

3 **If the objectives can be evaluated at the end of each session, when can the outcomes be measured?**

Activity

Reflect on the last PLD group session that you undertook. What was the aim of the session, and how did the objectives relate to the aim?

If you were to review the session, how might you change the aim and objectives set (if at all)?

5

Activities to enable personal learning and development

Learning Objectives

- Describe a range of activities for PLD group sessions
- Identify the benefits and pitfalls of each activity
- Clarify the resources required to enable the activity to take place
- Explain the relationship between the activities and the session objectives
- Describe how knowledge of learning styles informs the planning of activities

Introduction

The point has been reached in the planning process (and in this book) where the youth support worker can start to engage with the detailed content of the session. Deciding on appropriate activities for PLD sessions is, for many, the most enjoyable aspect of the planning process. It is at this point that the practitioner begins to consider what should happen during the session in order that young people leave the group having engaged in a personal learning and development experience. As Nelson-Jones asserts: 'As leaders you do not leave participants' skills development to chance. Instead you intentionally set up and manage activities that allow participants to understand, rehearse and practise targeted skills' (Nelson-Jones, 1991: 209).

This chapter continues to utilize the FAAST model as its foundation. Having identified a Focus (or topic) for the session (discussed in detail in Chapter 3), and set an appropriate Aim and related learning objectives (examined in Chapter 4), the youth support worker is ready to move on to consider relevant Activities for the session. The Structure is examined in detail in Chapter 6 and the Techniques are discussed in Chapter 7.

Having suggested that many youth support workers find selecting activities an enjoyable aspect of planning, it is important to be aware that the process can contain potential pitfalls. Caught up in the excitement of designing the activities with which participants will be involved during the session, there is a risk that key issues such as addressing the session objectives and taking account of learning theory and learning styles (examined in Chapter 2) may be overlooked. This chapter attends to these pitfalls, starting by setting out a range of activities and methods of delivery that can be used in PLD sessions. It considers the pros and cons of each, identifying the resources that different activities may require. The chapter goes on to examine how to select appropriate activities by building on the case study examples introduced in Chapters 3 and 4. In these earlier chapters, Lloyd, Ashraf, Crystal, Jatinder and Sam have each decided on a focus for their PLD sessions. They have also identified an aim and objectives for the session (which, it is planned, will lead to positive outcomes for the participants). It is now time to identify a range of activities that will enable participants to engage actively in the session and learn from it.

Activities and methods of delivery

Youth support workers who have delivered PLD group sessions will know that they have at their disposal a range of activities from which to select. The beauty of PLD sessions is that young people can be faced with creative and challenging learning experiences that may be unfamiliar to them, but which provide opportunities to learn more about themselves and help to make changes in their lives. The following list contains a selection of possible activities and methods of delivery:

- group discussion or debate;
- role play and simulation;
- games and quizzes;
- case studies and first-person narrative;
- participant research and presentations;
- art, music and drama;
- TV/DVD/film extracts;
- team-building activities;
- facilitator input/presentation.

Each of these activities is now examined in brief. The pros and cons are summarized and the resources required to ensure that the activity can be undertaken effectively are noted. Mindful of the limitations of exploring fully a range of activities in one chapter, suggestions for further reading about particular activities are made.

Group discussion or debate

A whole group discussion should involve all participants. It provides an opportunity to share and reflect on experiences that are critical to personal learning and development. It is the role of the youth support worker to pose key questions and to facilitate and summarize the discussions taking place.

Pros:

- Opportunity for all group members to engage with specific questions
- Opportunity to learn from the experiences and viewpoints of others
- Sharing experiences and ideas can be supportive and reduce feelings of isolation

Cons:

- Group members may feel excluded, particularly if English is not their first language or they are not confident in their communication skills
- Group members may feel intimidated, lack confidence in the group setting and be unwilling to contribute
- If the discussion lacks focus and is not adequately facilitated, it may not enable learning and development

Resources:

- A room that provides a conducive space for group discussion to take place (e.g. chairs set out in a circle)
- Questions or topics for discussion prepared in advance

Further reading

Killick, S. (2006) *Emotional Literacy at the Heart of the School Ethos*. London: Paul Chapman Publishing.

Tew, M., Read, M. and Potter, H. (2007) *Circles, PHSE and Citizenship: Assessing the Value of Circle Time in Secondary Schools*. London: Paul Chapman Publishing.

Role play and simulation

Role play and simulation, whereby young people adopt a role and act it out in a 'practise' scenario, provides an opportunity for participants to 'try out' a range of responses or skills. As long as the activity is undertaken in a safe and well-managed environment, role play and simulation can be an excellent way of learning and developing personal knowledge.

Pros:

- Opportunity to 'have a go' or practise something before experiencing it in a real-life situation
- Chance to experience how specific situations actually feel, examine responses to them and reflect on how they can be managed more effectively
- Role play can develop confidence and can be fun
- Observing other participants in role play or simulation settings can stimulate learning

Cons:

- Some participants may be reluctant to participate, particularly if the role play is being observed by the whole group. The facilitator does not want to get into a 'stand-off' situation with those young people who are not keen to take part!
- The activity could provide the opportunity for certain individuals to 'act up' or 'take centre stage' in a way that does not encourage learning for the group, and will require well-honed group management techniques from the facilitator
- Taking part in some practise situations may raise difficult or painful issues for participants who have experienced similar challenging situations in their own lives

Resources:

- A suitable 'space' in which the role play/simulation can take place
- Guidance on what the role play should focus on
- Preparation for a full debrief following the role play/simulation activity

Further reading

Brookfield, S. (2006) *The Skillful Teacher*. San Francisco, LA: Jossey-Bass.

Plummer, D.M. (2007) *Self-esteem Games for Children*. London: Jessica Kingsley.

Games and quizzes

Including games and quizzes in a personal learning and development session can encourage participation and foster an informal, positive and energetic learning environment. It is important, however, that the game or quiz links directly to the topic under discussion in the session and is not simply used to generate a sense of fun in the group.

Pros:

- Students feel motivated to participate
- An element of competition between small groups can focus thinking
- Learning can be 'disguised' and should be enjoyable and exciting, particularly for disengaged young people

Cons:

- Sessions can easily become noisy and 'out of control'
- Some young people may find it difficult to succeed or 'win' in the games/quizzes and thus lack confidence in participating. This could reinforce messages about 'failure'

- The 'fun' element of these activities may detract from the purpose of the session and learning may be limited

Resources:

- The 'space' in which the session takes place should be conducive to the game/s to be played. Seating should be arranged to provide opportunities to move around the room if appropriate
- Quiz sheets, instructions and any other resources connected with the game should be prepared and to hand

Further reading

Barlow, C., Blyth, J. and Edmonds, M. (1998) *A Handbook of Interactive Exercises for Groups*. Boston, MA: Allyn & Bacon.

Brandes, D. and Norris, J. (1998) *The Gamester's Handbook 3*. Cheltenham: Nelson Thornes.

Fuchs, B. (2002) *Group Games: Social Skills*. Bicester: Speechmark.

Case studies and first-person narratives

The use of case studies, where young people explore in a 'hypothetical' way, a scenario that may resonate with their own situations, can be helpful. Case studies encourage participants to 'think through' aspects of their lives, or circumstances in which they may find themselves in a safe way, via a third party. The use of first-person narratives, where the case study has been written with a 'real' voice telling a personal story, can put across issues, concerns and experiences that may be shared by group members powerfully. Through guided exploration of the narrative, ways of making sense of, and dealing with the issues, concerns and experiences, can be identified. This should then serve to illuminate thinking about future circumstances, choices and decisions.

Pros:

- Case studies or first-person narratives are engaged with easily. They feel 'real' and participants in the group should be able to relate to an aspect of the 'story'
- Opportunities will arise for discussion that does not focus solely on the 'story', but encourages future-oriented thinking and problem-solving
- Feelings of isolation may be reduced as participants become aware that others share their thoughts, feelings and uncertainties

Cons:

- Careful consideration must be given to writing the case studies, to ensure group members feel that their own needs are being recognized. A range of cultural and social backgrounds should be used that reflect those of the young people involved

- Youth support workers should be aware of the need to facilitate and support the work with case studies, to ensure that the emotional needs of individuals are recognized and met
- Case studies in written form may not be accessible to those with literacy needs or for whom English is not their first language

Resources:

- Preparation of written or pictorial case studies with key questions to stimulate discussion
- Adequate time to explore, and if necessary follow up the ideas, thoughts and feelings raised

Further reading

Amundson, N., Harris-Bowlesby, J. and Niles, S. (2008) *Essential Elements of Career Counselling: Processes and Technique*. Englewood Cliffs, NJ: Prentice Hall.

Reid, H.L. (2005) Narrative and career guidance: beyond small talk and towards useful dialogue for the 21st century, *International Journal for Vocational and Educational Guidance*, 5: 125–36.

Participant research and presentations to the group

Young people are likely to value information that they find out for themselves over information that is provided for them. Asking small groups to undertake research into a particular issue or topic as part of the session (as long as adequate materials and resources are easily accessible) can generate useful learning. Suggesting that those who have undertaken the research feed their ideas back to their peers in the group can be effective in helping young people to gain a range of skills including communication and confidence building.

Pros:

- All participants can be involved in accessing and researching information
- Young people will gather information about what is important to them (rather than what someone else thinks might be important!)
- Young people will develop research techniques alongside building confidence and communication skills when structuring and delivering a presentation to their peers

Cons:

- Young people might find the concept of researching information and giving presentations onerous or frightening

- Information may not be readily available or easily accessed by young people who have literacy or language support needs
- Using resources such as the internet may result in young people becoming distracted from the task in hand

Resources:

- A range of appropriate material/sources should be accessible in the session. These could include: books, magazines, internet, information about statutory or voluntary organizations and professional bodies
- Flip-chart paper and pens or other visual aids should be available for students to use when constructing their presentations
- Students may want to print or photocopy information as part of their presentations

Art, music and drama

Providing young people with opportunities to express their thoughts, ideas and feelings using a creative medium can be an exciting and liberating experience. Students often feel constrained in saying what they want to say in front of peers. The use of drama, dance, art or music in the session, which encourages young people to collaborate, will not only offer the chance for students to express themselves, but will provide an opportunity to work with others, taking risks, building relationships of trust and listening to each other. The end result, it is hoped, is that confidence is increased, trust in their peers is established and thoughts and feelings are expressed.

Pros:

- Group members have the opportunity to develop their thinking and express their feelings in a safe and creative environment
- The creative arts are often central to the lives of adolescents. Therefore, they will be motivated to use activities like song writing, poster design, choreographing or drama effectively
- In-depth personal learning and development can be achieved if young people are collaborating with other students, are given freedom and responsibility with a project and are encouraged to produce a piece of work as an end result

Cons:

- Some young people may find it difficult to 'join in' if they feel they lack creative or artistic skills
- Not all youth support workers feel comfortable managing creative activities if they do not share some expertise in these areas
- Engagement in the task may mean that there is a risk of losing sight of the personal

learning and development in favour of giving Oscar-winning performances, or trying to become the next 'Big Thing' in the world of celebrity

Resources:

- Space in which to undertake creative activities
- Tools, including paper, pens, glue, magazines, props, musical instruments, basic recording equipment and other creative resources

Further reading

Clifford, S. and Herrmann, A. (1999) *Making a Leap: Theatre of Empowerment*. London: Jessica Kingsley.

Draley, S. and Heath, W. (2007) *The Expressive Arts Activity Book: A Resource for Professionals*. London: Jessica Kingsley.

Jennings, S. (1986) *Creative Drama in Groupwork*. Bicester: Winslow Press.

Liebmann, M. (2008) *Art Therapy for Groups: A Handbook of Themes and Exercises*, 2nd edn. Hove: Brunner-Routledge.

TV, DVD, programmes/films/extracts

It can be helpful to use extracts from DVDs or TV programmes as a starting point for discussion or to illustrate specific scenarios. Young people usually engage easily with visual images, and they will be familiar with watching programmes and films for recreation and enjoyment. As long as the youth support worker is clear about why the particular programme or film clip will be useful to the topic under discussion, then this can be a useful and thought-provoking learning resource.

Pros:

- TV is a familiar media to young people and one with which they will engage
- There are some stimulating programmes available, rich in content for discussion
- Clips can be stopped and started as appropriate allowing for discussion and other activities at key points to broaden and consolidate learning

Cons:

- If the film/clip/programme is not seen as being relevant or up to date, then all credibility will be lost and the group are unlikely to engage with the content (and more likely to become distracted by the out-of-date hair-dos!)
- If the youth support worker has not watched the film/clip/programme carefully first, the usefulness and learning potential will be diminished
- Timings need to be managed carefully. A one-hour PLD session that is taken up with a 50-minute TV programme may seem like a gift to a nervous or inexperienced youth support worker, but it will not enable personal learning and development as

effectively as a session with several short clips that can be stopped and discussed in detail
- Copyright issues may need to be checked

Resources:

- Appropriate technical equipment (and knowledge of how to operate it)
- TV programmes, films, DVDs
- Prepared activities or discussion points

Team-building activities

Learning by working with others in a team can be effective in helping young people to discover more about themselves. As well as encouraging increased self-awareness, it also develops other communication, team working and leadership skills. It is the function of the youth support worker to set up the activity and then take the role of observer rather than facilitator. Observations are shared at the end of the activity to encourage students to reflect on how they worked together in a team setting.

Pros:

- Team-building activities can be stimulating and engaging
- Learning more about 'self' and relating to others can take place
- Transferable skills such as communication and leadership are developed

Cons:

- Some young people may feel intimidated or overwhelmed within a team
- There may be a risk of bullying behaviour if dominant group members 'take control'
- If the activity is not properly debriefed, learning may be lost

Resources:

- Team-building activities take time to develop. A half-day or one-day workshop would be ideal
- Depending on the activity, it is likely that the youth support worker may need to gather together a range of resources. Often team-building activities are centred on constructing an object or a machine, or transporting something from A to B. It is the responsibility of the youth support worker to ensure that the resources are available in order for the activity to be carried out

Further reading

Johnson, D.W. and Johnson, F.P. (1997) *Joining Together: Group Theory and Group Skills*, 6th edn. Boston, MA: Allyn & Bacon.

Facilitator input/presentations

Although PLD sessions should involve the young people actively in their learning, there will be times when the youth support worker will want to input information to the group. When information is presented well, the group's knowledge and understanding will be broadened. If done ineffectively (with the youth support worker mumbling apologetically or hiding behind the flip-chart), the young people may feel bored and disengaged, which could lead to displays of disruptive behaviour in the session.

Pros:

- Relevant information can be delivered in a helpful and accessible way
- The information will be accurate and free from bias or stereotyping
- The youth support worker will be viewed as someone with knowledge and expertise who is there to help and support

Cons:

- Students may become bored or restless if they are not involved
- If presentations are made using visual aids that rely on the written word, the information may not be accessible to all group members (e.g. those with literacy needs or those for whom English is not their first language). Similarly, pictorial images should reflect the ethnic and cultural diversity within the group
- A clear and engaging delivery is essential to ensure that the group members remain interested, coupled with an understanding of any technology to be used in the presentation

Resources:

- Visual aids (flip-charts, interactive white boards, PowerPoint presentations)
- Access to technology if required
- Up-to-date and accurate information to present to the group

Further reading

Bradbury, A. (2006) *Successful Presentation Skills*, 3rd edn. London: Kogan Page.

The activities and methods of delivery outlined above are likely to form the basic menu from which to select. However, this is by no means an exhaustive list, and youth support workers are encouraged to consult with colleagues and other professionals to access the range of resources available in order to broaden their repertoire of activities.

It would be remiss, when focusing on activities and methods of delivery, not to mention the need to be mindful of the concept of differentiation. In any one group, young people are likely to present with different levels of ability and learning needs (as well as a range of learning styles). It is important to ensure that these have been taken into account when designing the activities. If, for example, there is a wide range of abilities within the group, then activities should be extended or simplified as appropriate.

Activity

Reflect on the list of activities and methods of delivery outlined and consider ways in which you could adapt them for a group with widely differing ability levels.

Now that there is an awareness of the range of possible activities that can be used in PLD sessions, it is important to establish how these methods of delivery relate to:

- theories underpinning learning;
- session objectives.

The relationship between activities, learning theory and learning styles

In Chapter 2 of this book the concepts of experiential learning (Kolb, 1984), student-centred learning (Brandes and Ginnis, 1996) and learning styles (Gardner, 1993; Honey and Mumford, 2000) were examined. It was suggested that individuals learn from their experiences (experiential learning) and should be encouraged to be an active participant in their learning (student-centred learning), but that they also learn in a variety of ways (learning styles). First, if we are to accept that young people learn by reflecting on their own experiences and those of others, then activities which encourage the sharing of experiences, or even structuring of new experiences, will encourage personal learning and development to take place. A group discussion or a team-building activity, for example, provides an excellent opportunity to involve students in learning by experience. Second, to encourage students to be active participants in their learning, youth support workers should select engaging and interactive methods of delivery. This might involve offering a 'menu' of activities to ensure that every participant feels challenged and involved in the session. Use of creative activities such as drama, music and art are effective ways of engaging all group members in their learning. Finally, knowledge of the concept of learning styles should also inform the selection of activities in PLD sessions. Being mindful of the different ways in which individuals learn should encourage youth support workers to select activities that appeal, as far as possible, across a range of learning styles.

The relationship between activities and learning theory and learning styles cannot be overstated. If practitioners fail to take account of the theory underpinning learning and individual learning preferences, the session is at risk of disengaging the participants and failing to offer them experiences from which they can learn.

When faced with selecting appropriate activities to use in PLD sessions, youth support workers may find themselves drawn to particular activities. This is not in itself a 'bad' thing. However, it may be that the activities concerned relate to the particular learning preference of the youth support worker. For example, a youth support worker with a dominant 'activist' learning style may be tempted to structure a whole session on a role play/simulation activity. This will, of course, appeal to their own learning style and to 'activist' young people in the group, but may risk excluding reflectors and theorists. Knowledge of our own learning style is important in order to ensure that we do not allow our own preferences to dominate the session.

The relationship between session objectives and activities

As has already been made clear, there is a chronology to planning PLD sessions that begins with assessing the needs of the group and establishing an appropriate Focus to the session, followed by setting a relevant Aim and related objectives. The next step in the process is to select from a range of possible Activities. There are links between each stage of the process, and the partnership between the Aim, the session objectives, and the Activities is crucial. The need for specific and verifiable session objectives is made clear in the previous chapter. Undertaking relevant activities during the session ensures that the objectives are met. For example, if objectives require participants to 'state', 'draw', 'write', 'describe', 'identify', 'explain', and so on, the activities planned for those sessions should provide the opportunity for students to do just that.

This example outlines an appropriate and an inappropriate activity for a specific objective.

Objective: Participants have the opportunity to (PHOTO)

Describe a recent experience where they used effective communication skills

Appropriate activity:

In small groups or with a partner, share a recent experience where communication skills were used effectively. Write down what made this communication effective. Feed your points back to the whole group.

Inappropriate activity:

Complete a true/false quiz that details a range of statements concerning effective communication skills.

The first activity in the example directly addresses the session objective. By sharing their experiences with a partner or in a small group and feeding back key points about their communication skills, students have the opportunity to 'describe a recent experience where they used effective communication skills'. In the second example, although the activity relates to effective communication skills, it does not directly address the objective set and students would not necessarily share their own 'recent experiences' as the objective dictates.

In order to apply the key concepts introduced in this chapter to practice, we will return to Lloyd, Ashraf, Crystal, Jatinder and Sam. So far, each youth support worker has had the opportunity to assess the needs of the group with whom they are working and to set a Focus for the session. They have also identified a session Aim, and, in most cases, established relevant objectives. They are now considering the activities they might use, mindful of the pros and cons, the resources they require, learning theory, and the need to ensure that the session objectives are met. To start, we will return to Lloyd's 45-minute session for eight 15-year-olds.

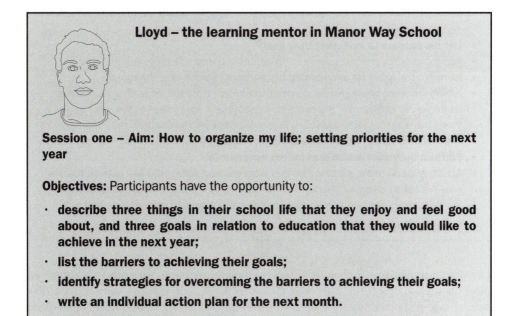

Lloyd – the learning mentor in Manor Way School

Session one – Aim: How to organize my life; setting priorities for the next year

Objectives: Participants have the opportunity to:

· **describe three things in their school life that they enjoy and feel good about, and three goals in relation to education that they would like to achieve in the next year;**
· **list the barriers to achieving their goals;**
· **identify strategies for overcoming the barriers to achieving their goals;**
· **write an individual action plan for the next month.**

Lloyd begins his consideration of suitable activities by taking each of the objectives in turn and identifying possible activities that will ensure they are met. Once he has a list of potential activities that he knows will directly address each objective, he must consider the pros/cons of each, and examine the resources he will need. In addition, Lloyd asks himself the following questions:

1   Overall, is the session student-centred? Do participants have the opportunity to engage in, and take responsibility for their learning?
2   Is the session experiential? Are there opportunities for students to share and learn from their experiences?
3   Are a range of learning styles catered for in the session?

Lloyd is confident that the activities he chooses will provide a stimulating, but balanced approach to his PLD session. In the following example, the objectives and the corresponding activities that Lloyd has decided upon are identified.

- **Describe three things in their school life that they enjoy and feel good about, and three goals in relation to education that they would like to achieve in the next year**
- Activity: *Individually, compile a list of aspects of their school life that they feel good about and enjoy. Share these with a partner and, following discussion, agree the three most important. Working as a whole group, identify and discuss a range of goals in relation to education that young people of their age could achieve. Back to working in pairs to each agree the three goals that they would like to achieve in the next year.*
- **List the barriers to achieving their goals**
- Activity: *In small groups, make a list of potential barriers to achieving their goals*
- **Identify strategies for overcoming the barriers to achieving their goals**
- Activity: *In same small groups, choose two barriers from the list and agree possible strategies for overcoming the barriers. Present these ideas back to the other group. (Note: the way that these ideas are presented back can be creative and can involve role play, art, music, and other presentation skills).*
- **Write an individual action plan for the next month**
- Activity: *Return to the partner that they were working with in the first activity, discuss possible action steps for the next month (relating to the three key goals identified in the first activity). Individually, complete a simple action plan proforma, setting out action steps for the next month.*

Lloyd is confident that each activity will provide participants with the opportunity to meet the session objectives. He is also clear that the session invites students to participate, to take responsibility for their own learning and incorporates a range of learning styles. Most importantly, he knows that each activity provides participants with the opportunity to reflect on *themselves* and *their own position* in relation to the topic, which is central to PLD group work. Lloyd's only concern focuses on resources. He is aware that he will need to prepare key materials (such as action plan proformas) and he should also provide pens, paper and flip-charts for the groups to present back their ideas. None of this is a problem. What Lloyd is more concerned about, in relation to resources, is whether he has 'overloaded' the session (45 minutes is not long once the young people have taken time to arrive and settled themselves ready to work). However, Lloyd decides to go ahead with the next step in the planning process (establishing the structure for the session), which is examined in detail in Chapter 6.

Like Lloyd, Ashraf is also ready to plan the activities he would like to use in his session. He will be working with a class of 13-year-olds in the school and has been allocated a one-hour slot in which to introduce the students to the range of support that is available to them both within the school and outside of it.

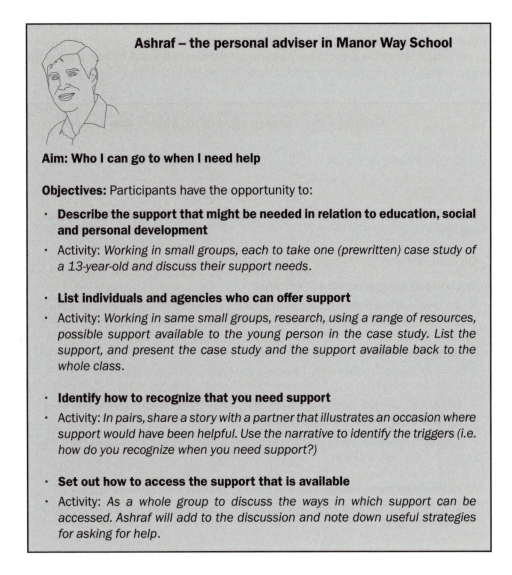

Ashraf – the personal adviser in Manor Way School

Aim: Who I can go to when I need help

Objectives: Participants have the opportunity to:

- **Describe the support that might be needed in relation to education, social and personal development**
- Activity: *Working in small groups, each to take one (prewritten) case study of a 13-year-old and discuss their support needs.*

- **List individuals and agencies who can offer support**
- Activity: *Working in same small groups, research, using a range of resources, possible support available to the young person in the case study. List the support, and present the case study and the support available back to the whole class.*

- **Identify how to recognize that you need support**
- Activity: *In pairs, share a story with a partner that illustrates an occasion where support would have been helpful. Use the narrative to identify the triggers (i.e. how do you recognize when you need support?)*

- **Set out how to access the support that is available**
- Activity: *As a whole group to discuss the ways in which support can be accessed. Ashraf will add to the discussion and note down useful strategies for asking for help.*

Ashraf is confident that he has linked the activities to the session objectives. He is also aware that he will need to prepare a range of resources; in particular, materials he can share with the group when they are researching different sources of support available. He has checked that the room he is teaching in has internet access that can be used as part of this research process. Ashraf will also write the individual case studies, mindful of ensuring that the scenarios he presents will be relevant to the group of young people with whom he is working, taking into account the ethnic, social and cultural background of the students. Reflecting on his knowledge of learning theory, Ashraf feels that the activities he has chosen are appropriate to young people with a range of different learning styles. In particular, the use of case studies will engage activists, pragmatists and reflectors and the research activity linked to the case studies will involve the theorists in the group. Much of the learning is experiential and will engage students as it bears relevance to their own situations.

Crystal is undergoing the same planning process with her lunch-time session for young people who are considering moving on from school to Higher Education.

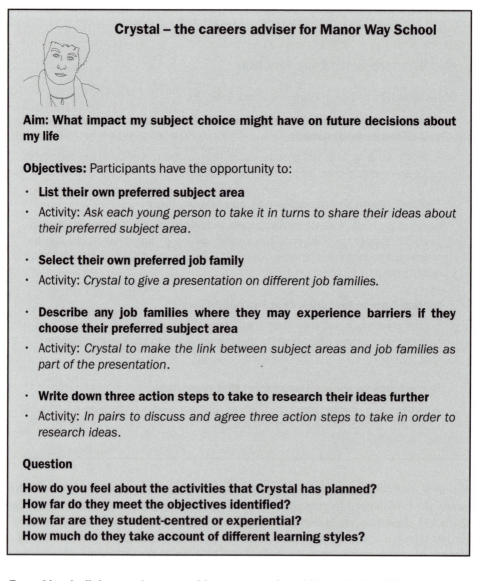

Crystal – the careers adviser for Manor Way School

Aim: What impact my subject choice might have on future decisions about my life

Objectives: Participants have the opportunity to:

- **List their own preferred subject area**
- Activity: *Ask each young person to take it in turns to share their ideas about their preferred subject area.*

- **Select their own preferred job family**
- Activity: *Crystal to give a presentation on different job families.*

- **Describe any job families where they may experience barriers if they choose their preferred subject area**
- Activity: *Crystal to make the link between subject areas and job families as part of the presentation.*

- **Write down three action steps to take to research their ideas further**
- Activity: *In pairs to discuss and agree three action steps to take in order to research ideas.*

Question
How do you feel about the activities that Crystal has planned?
How far do they meet the objectives identified?
How far are they student-centred or experiential?
How much do they take account of different learning styles?

Crystal has built her session around her presentation. Although she will be imparting helpful and relevant information, she is not taking account of the principles of PLD sessions (i.e. that young people have the opportunity to reflect on their own position in relation to the topic). In addition, the activities planned do not address the objectives. For example, one objective stipulates that participants will have the opportunity to *write down three action steps*, yet the related activity does not involve writing at all. The use of a presentation by Crystal in this case is neither student-centred nor experiential. Of course, it is important where appropriate for youth support workers to input and share information during PLD sessions, but they should not be tempted to 'take over'. Finally, Crystal has not given individual learning styles enough thought. The activists and pragmatists in the group may feel disengaged during her presentation and those who have a kinaesthetic, intrapersonal, spatial, mathematical or creative preference for learning may be at a disadvantage. However, Crystal is unaware of these potential limitations, and goes ahead with her planning. We revisit Crystal in Chapter 6 as she structures her session in detail.

Jatinder has also started to prepare her PLD session. She has decided on the aim for her first session with the four young students in the school who are pregnant. Jatinder has been given two hours each week to support the young women as a group, and to help them to explore a range of issues relating to their pregnancy and childbirth needs.

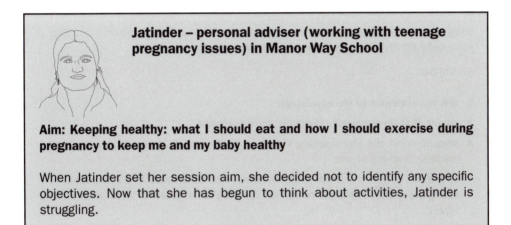

Jatinder – personal adviser (working with teenage pregnancy issues) in Manor Way School

Aim: Keeping healthy: what I should eat and how I should exercise during pregnancy to keep me and my baby healthy

When Jatinder set her session aim, she decided not to identify any specific objectives. Now that she has begun to think about activities, Jatinder is struggling.

Jatinder decides that she will ask the group how they would like to tackle the subject of healthy eating and exercise by starting with a group discussion. She prepares some handouts on recommended amounts of protein, carbohydrates, fats and vitamins in the diet to keep healthy during pregnancy should they be needed. Apart from this, Jatinder does not have time to prepare any further resources or activities. She decides to 'go with the flow' and 'play it by ear', meeting the needs of the group members as they become apparent through the group discussion.

Question

How might Jatinder's lack of preparation have an impact on the PLD session?

Although in many ways Jatinder is taking a truly student-centred approach to the session by placing responsibility for their learning with the group members, she is not providing any learning opportunities other than a group discussion. In a two-hour session this is unlikely to keep the group engaged. Furthermore, there is the risk that some of the young women in the group may feel reluctant to 'speak out' in front of their peers, and could feel inhibited. Although Jatinder is clear that she does not have time to go through the planning process in detail, what becomes apparent is that she is taking a risk with the two hours that she has available to work with these young women. As a result of her lack of planning the participants may feel that they have achieved very little and their personal learning and development may be non-existent.

In the final case study example, Sam, the youth worker, is preparing a one-hour PLD session for a group of 14- to 16-year-old young men. You will recall that in Chapter 4 you assisted Sam by suggesting an aim and objectives for his session. Now appropriate activities must be identified.

Activity

Using the session aim and objectives you identified in Chapter 4, continue the planning process by deciding on suitable activities for the session.

Remember:

1 **link the activities to the objectives;**

2 **ensure that the resources (time etc.) are available;**

3 **keep in mind the key learning theories: student-centred learning, experiential learning, learning styles;**

4 **and don't forget ... PLD group work needs to provide the opportunity for individual group members to reflect on their own position in relation to the topic.**

Summary

Deciding on appropriate methods of delivery for PLD sessions involves far more than simply choosing some 'fun' activities, put together to ensure that the session is action-packed. Youth support workers will need to select carefully, demonstrating that they are mindful of the objectives they have set for the session. Each activity has pros and cons, and an evaluation of these should be undertaken to ensure that the method of delivery is appropriate. The ability levels within the group should be considered so that differentiation within the activities can be planned. Finally, attention should be paid to learning theory and learning styles to ensure that all group members have the opportunity to engage in and learn from the session.

It is important that regardless of how relevant, stimulating and challenging the activities are, the role of youth support workers remains to ensure that the session works as a structured whole (see Chapter 6). Furthermore, without the skills and techniques necessary to facilitate learning, it makes little difference how much preparation has gone into the activities. It is the role of youth support workers to use their skills to encourage group members to engage with and learn from the activities that have been planned. These techniques and skills are discussed in Chapter 7.

Questions

The following questions and suggested activity will assist reflection on the key themes addressed in this chapter:

1 **What is the relationship between activities and learning theory (in particular experiential learning, student-centred learning and individual learning styles)?**
2 **How should activities relate to the session objectives?**
3 **Reflect on the last PLD session that you undertook. How far did the activities meet the range of learning styles in the group? How far did the activities undertaken ensure that the session objectives were met? If you were to review the session, how might you amend or develop the activities?**

6

Getting the structure of sessions right

Learning Objectives

- Identify a framework for structuring PLD sessions
- Explain the role of the youth support worker in managing the structure
- Engage with the detail of session planning
- Produce a detailed session plan for a PLD session

Introduction

In previous chapters the planning process for PLD group sessions is explored, utilizing the FAAST model to inform the chronology and detail of the preparation. First, the importance of establishing a **Focus** for each PLD session is made clear, based on a broad assessment of the needs of group members. Second, once the focus has been agreed, the youth support worker decides on an appropriate **Aim** or 'title' for the session that determines a sense of direction and purpose. The aim links to verifiable session objectives, whereby participants have the opportunity to **(PHOTO)** achieve a number of predetermined objectives within the session. Third, to ensure that the session aim and objectives are achieved, the youth support worker needs to select appropriate **Activities** to undertake during the session. These activities should be chosen carefully, drawing on knowledge of learning theory (experiential and student-centred learning perspectives) and learning styles, while at the same time taking account of the range of ability levels and diversity within the group. The youth support worker now has a clear sense of what the session is setting out to achieve, and what methods will be employed in the group work to ensure that PLD takes place. This is all good, but the planning process is not yet complete. It is now the responsibility of the youth support worker to ensure that the session has a **Structure** in place that enables PLD to be maximized.

This chapter focuses on the 'structuring' aspect of the planning process. It begins by suggesting a 'framework' on which the session can be built effectively. It goes on to clarify the part that the youth support worker plays in ensuring that the session remains flexible, but focused, providing the participants with a clear and logical progression towards meeting the learning objectives. Furthermore, it suggests a format that can be used to plan and record the structure, timings, and activities, and identify the resources that are required. Once again, Lloyd, Ashraf, Crystal, Jatinder and Sam add clarity to the process by illustrating what is involved in developing a session in practice.

What is structure and why is it necessary in PLD sessions?

Most youth support workers will be aware of the part that 'structure' plays in their helping interactions with young people. In their one-to-one work, for example, interventions are likely to be structured in such a way that young people have the opportunity to identify the issues and concerns they are facing, explore strategies for addressing these and plan action that will ensure that the strategies are put into place. These interventions are more than simply 'cosy chats'. They are focused on working towards positive outcomes for young people and therefore it is important that they remain structured and purposeful. The same principles apply to group interventions. Geldard and Geldard make the case for structure in group work:

> It is sensible to design each session so that the programme flows smoothly from one activity to another and maintains interest and energy while continuing to address the relevant theme or topic.
>
> (Geldard and Geldard, 2001: 67)

The importance of ensuring that the structure focuses on the 'relevant theme or topic' and does not drift away from the subject into unrelated areas is emphasized by Malekoff:

> Too often what a group does has nothing to do with where it's headed. Instead, what it does is to keep the group busy and the practitioner free of anxiety. It is essential that content and purpose are integrally connected.
>
> (Malekoff, 2004: 82)

If there is little or no structure to the session, then it is likely that one or more of the consequences outlined below may result:

- Young people may be unaware of what the session is all about and how it is relevant to them.
- Activities may be disjointed, lack clarity and appear to be unrelated to the topic.
- Personal learning and development may be limited.
- Group members may become disinterested and distracted.
- Management and 'control' of the session may become an issue.

- The session may lack momentum and impetus.
- The session may over or under-run the allocated time.
- There is little to build on in subsequent PLD sessions.
- The credibility of the youth support worker is diminished.

If, however, the youth support worker attends to the structure of the session in planning, then the consequences outlined above are unlikely to result and the group session will be successful in the following ways:

- Young people will have a clear understanding of what the session is about and how it will be useful to them.
- Group members will feel motivated to participate, knowing what they are doing and why they are doing it.
- Activities will link, flow and build one to another.
- The youth support worker is able to draw threads between the activities, thus contributing to building on the personal learning and development of group members.

So, if structure is a 'good thing', what should it look like and what models or frameworks can we use to inform the structuring of PLD sessions?

Structuring the session – a framework

Having already established that many youth support workers adopt a structured approach (albeit one that can be used flexibly) in their one-to-one interventions with young people, a useful starting point for considering how to structure group sessions is to reflect on the concepts and frameworks that practitioners use in their one-to-one work and 'test out' the applicability of these to the group context. A key model for engaging and working with clients that is used widely throughout the 'helping professions' (including youth support work) is Gerard Egan's (2002) 'skilled helper' approach. In brief, Egan's approach to problem management suggests a structured, yet flexible way to engage and work with clients. This purposeful helping process is described by Egan as a three-stage model where stage one focuses on helping clients to identify their problems ('current scenario'), stage two enables them to consider possibilities and strategies for change, identifying realistic goals that they want to achieve ('preferred scenario') and stage three focuses on planning action to ensure that the goals are reached ('getting there'). Although the 'three stages' of the model imply a linear progression through a helping interaction, Egan makes clear that the model should be used flexibly and over time. So, how useful might this structure be as a framework for PLD group sessions? In the case of group work, it is important that each session is structured in such a way as to optimize personal learning and development, while at the same time allowing for flexibility in approach. Egan's model emphasizes this flexibility at its core. However, each PLD session should also be planned for delivery as a 'stand-alone' intervention, with a clear sense of beginning, middle and end, even if the session forms one of a number of PLD group works. This will ensure that individual sessions are purposeful and of value in achieving positive outcomes for those involved.

Reid and Fielding (2007) draw on Egan's three-stage model in developing their single interaction model (SIM) that recognizes the value of structure in helping interactions with young people. But they go further in that the model they have developed acknowledges the significance of structure in every interaction with young people, even if the intervention is a 'one-off' meeting. Like Egan's model, the SIM encompasses three stages:

- Stage one – negotiating the contract and agreeing the agenda.
- Stage two – developing issues and identifying goals.
- Stage three – designing, planning and implementing action.

And, like Egan's three-stage model, it has been designed specifically for one-to-one interventions. But it makes sense to consider how a helping model such as this might inform not only one-to-one work, but group sessions too.

The three stages of the SIM model, when transposed to the group setting, involve:

- sharing the focus of the session with participants and encouraging them to see its relevance;
- undertaking a range of activities to gain a deeper understanding of the topic and how it relates to them;
- encouraging group members to summarize their learning and plan action steps for the future.

Table 6.1 provides an overview of what should be included in each of the three stages in a PLD session, and shows how the model can be simplified by describing stage one as the beginning, stage two as the middle and stage three as the end of the session.

All stages of the model have equal significance, although there are features of each which are worthy of note and further exploration. The role of the youth support worker in managing the structure of the session is critical. Both the stages themselves and the role of the practitioner in managing them are examined in more depth.

The role of the youth support worker in managing the structure

Stage one

It is important that the PLD session gets off to a positive start. If stage one is managed effectively and the students are clear about why they are there, what they are going to be doing and how the session will be of value to them, then the battle to engage their interest and 'grab' their attention is largely won. Although time would have been invested by the youth support worker in the planning stages, ensuring that the topic is one that is relevant to the group and meets their needs (assessing needs and identifying

Table 6.1 A three-stage model for group work

Stage one – negotiating the contract and agreeing an agenda (the beginning)
- Welcome the group
- Introduce yourself (if this a first session) and ask group members to introduce themselves (this could involve undertaking an 'ice-breaker' activity)
- Introduce the topic, and, if appropriate, explain the aims and objectives for the session
- Help the group to see how/why the topic is relevant to them at this point in their lives
- Check out what the group knows already about the topic
- Agree with the group the broad content that the session will cover
- Agree with the group a contract or set of 'ground roles' for the session

Stage two – developing issues and identifying goals (the middle)
- Engage with activities in order to explore the topic in detail
- Encourage interaction and participation by all group members
- Input information as necessary
- Encourage individual group members to reflect on their own position in relation to the topic
- Provide opportunities for individual decision making in relation to the topic

Stage three – designing, planning and implementing action (the end)
- Encourage group members to summarize the key themes addressed in the session
- Provide the opportunity in the session for each group member to plan action in relation to the topic
- Formalize the action planning process where possible
- Provide opportunities for individual group members to reflect on their learning
- Encourage group members to evaluate the session. How useful have they found it and what are they going to do as a result?
- Thank the group and end

---

topics is discussed in detail in Chapter 3); it is nevertheless important to avoid making assumptions about the groups' prior knowledge in relation to the topic. By the end of stage one, group members should be clear about what the focus of the session is, what they are hoping to achieve as a result, what they will be doing during the session (an overview), the 'tone' of the session (interactive, participative and experiential), the role of the facilitator and the ground rules (or contract) agreed by the group.

Setting an open, friendly, but purposeful tone is key to the session's success and this should be established from the outset. The room should be set up appropriately and, wherever possible, the youth support worker should arrive before the group members to ensure that the environment is conducive to PLD taking place. It may be that chairs are moved, or tables are pushed to one side in order to minimize the appearance of a 'classroom' and replace it with a 'personal learning and development environment'. Youth support workers should place themselves in the room to welcome group members as they arrive, thus sending the message 'I am open, I am approachable, I am here for you, I want to work with you, I am organized and prepared and I have positive expectations of you and the way in which you will engage with this session'. If this is the first time that the youth support workers have met with the groups, or if the groups are large ones (class-sized, for example), they may want to emphasize the 'firm but fair' approach. This gives a clear indication to participants that the session will be well managed and boundaried. It also provides 'space' for the youth support workers to relax their approach during the session as the relationship with the group builds.

Like one-to-one interactions, it is important that group members are encouraged to be involved from the outset. A long introduction from the facilitator in the early stages may serve to 'switch off' group members, whereas an introductory exercise where each group member has the opportunity to be involved will set an interactive tone for the session. Where possible, it is important that the introductory activity is linked to the topic. For example, if the session focuses on 'decision making', a possible activity would involve asking individual group members to introduce themselves and talk about the last item of clothing they bought, explaining how they arrived at this decision. In responding, these group members are illustrating a decision they made and identifying the factors that contributed to the decision-making process. This provides the facilitator with the opportunity to introduce the topic and expand on it further.

Once the topic is introduced, the next step is to help the group to see how the subject is relevant to them at this point in their lives. Engaging in a dialogue with questions such as 'what do you think made me choose this topic?' 'how might it be useful to you at this point?' 'why might this topic have an impact on your life in the near future?' and so on helps to focus and engage the participants. It is important that this conversation takes place and that it is not rushed. Investing time in clarifying how the session is relevant to the group members will reap rewards as the young people 'buy in' to the topic, recognizing its significance to them. Once there is recognition of the value of the subject, it is crucial to 'check out' the young people's existing knowledge. Have they talked about it before? Have they had any other sessions with a similar focus? If the answer is 'yes' the facilitator must explore further by establishing what group members know and understand about the topic. By so doing, the youth support worker can build on the group's prior knowledge and avoid duplicating it.

One further task for stage one is to agree a 'contract' or set of 'ground rules' with the group. Doel explains:

> The ground rules are rather like the constitution for the group – a statement of mutual expectations, an agreement about what is acceptable and not acceptable, and possibly what sanctions may be invoked if they are breached. Negotiating the ground rules is a demonstration of care for group processes.
>
> (Doel, 2006: 69)

In PLD group work, the negotiation of ground rules is a clear indicator that PLD sessions are different to being in a classroom. The facilitator is encouraging group members to become active participants, to share with each other ideas for making the session 'safe'. The ground rules may include practical elements like 'no mobile phones' and 'listening to each other' and 'not talking over each other', but they should also focus on more abstract concepts such as 'treating each other with respect' and 'confidentiality'. The ground rules should be discussed fully so that meaning is explicit, and they should be written down and displayed in each session. Whenever a group member or the facilitator feels that the rules are being contravened in some way, they can refer back to what was agreed by the group at the outset and restate or renegotiate if necessary.

In summary, what should be apparent is that stage one is crucial in setting the tone, introducing the topic and encouraging the group to take responsibility for, and share in their learning. Done well, the group will be engaged, keen to learn more and motivated to take an active part in the remainder of the session. When a hasty or piecemeal approach is taken, the group is likely to be unfocused, disparate, disengaged or, at worst, disruptive. If the introduction is laboured and ponderous, interest will be lost. So, pause, take time and a thoughtful stage one should lead to success in the stages that follow.

Stage two

Where stage one has established what the session is about, what it is setting out to achieve and how the individual participants will be involved, stage two goes on to provide the young people with opportunities to develop their knowledge and understanding of the topic further. Now the youth support worker is able to facilitate the activities they have planned that provide participants with the opportunity to gain an in-depth understanding of the topic. The role of the youth support worker at this stage is to explain the activities clearly, to ensure that the resources are available, to manage the activities and to make links and draw threads between them, thus encouraging reflection and learning. Skills and techniques for introducing, facilitating and managing activities is examined in detail in Chapter 7, but it is important to emphasize at this point the need to give instructions clearly and precisely, and to invite group members to repeat what they have been asked to do in order to ensure that there is clarity about what the activity involves.

It is also critical that the youth support worker takes part in facilitating the activities, remaining watchful for any individuals who are finding it difficult to engage or are unclear about what they are being asked to do. The facilitator should also be alert to individuals who are completing activities very quickly and who may become disengaged and distract others as a result. Alternatively, some young people may take significantly longer to complete an activity and it may help to condense or simplify the task in order to gain optimum learning. The need to be mindful of differentiation in the group is critical, particularly if the youth support worker is meeting the group for the first time and is not familiar with the abilities and any additional needs of the individual participants.

The task of the facilitator at this stage in the process is to make links between the activities and encourage participants to think about their own personal learning and development in relation to the topic. Some youth support workers may lack confidence in their ability to facilitate reflection by summarizing key points, inviting feedback and taking 'centre stage' in managing discussions. They may prefer to progress speedily from one activity to another; for example, 'now that you have finished discussing the case studies, go on and do the role play'. This will ensure that participants are constantly involved and busy, but will result in losing the opportunity to process and reflect on what they are learning. An alternative approach might be 'now that you have explored the case studies in your groups, let's share the key issues that you talked about together?' or 'how might what you have found out as a result of the case studies have an impact on a decision you make in the future?' It is by engaging in thoughtful reflection and discussion, sharing experiences and ideas, that personal learning and development will take place. This may not necessarily result in an 'a-ha' moment of revelation for the young people involved, but it will, it is hoped, contribute to their understanding about issues that are impacting on their lives.

The purpose of this stage then is threefold:

1 Develop a greater understanding of the topic.

2 Enable individuals to reflect on their own position in relation to the topic.

3 Engage in and learn from the group process.

In addition to attending to the topic, and the personal learning and development of each group member, the role of the facilitator is to encourage the development of the group itself. The group should now be forging an identity of its own in which the dynamic is positive and the young people feel safe, take responsibility and learn (group dynamics is discussed in detail in Chapter 8). By the end of stage two, group members will have had the chance to explore the topic fully, gain a greater understanding of it, reflect on their own position in relation to it, and begin to feel they 'belong' in the group. So, how does stage three build on this learning?

Stage three

Like stage one, stage three can often become rushed. Where stage two has focused on developing a greater understanding of self in relation to a topic, stage three attempts to translate this understanding into action. Put simply, it asks group members to consider what they intend to do as a result of their enhanced knowledge of a particular subject. For example, if a PLD session focuses on 'developing communication skills', participants should be introduced to the concept of communication skills in stage one. In stage two they will identify what constitutes communication skills and why they are important, and they will have gone on to consider their own strengths and areas for development in relation to communicating. At the end of stage two, each group member should be clear about the communication skills they use effectively and those they wish to develop further. Stage three then is all about planning ways in which they can build on and develop these skills.

As is the case in one-to-one interactions where the youth support worker and young person will take time to plan action in the session, the same should apply to PLD group work. The youth support worker should structure activities in stage three that are forward-focused and centre on planning the specific action that each group member needs to take. This action should lead to positive outcomes for the session (discussed in Chapter 4), whereby the young people will leave knowing what they must do, why they should do it, when they should do it by and what support they might require. Where the PLD session is one of a number of group meetings, the youth support worker will have the opportunity to 'follow up' the action taken in subsequent sessions.

Stage three also provides the young people with the opportunity to evaluate the session (evaluation is looked at in detail in Chapter 10). This means 'checking out' with the group how useful they have found the session, what have they learned, what has gone well, which activities they gained most from, what they would have added or changed, and how they would like to build on their learning in any subsequent sessions. And, of course, any session should end by ensuring that group members have access to further support should they need it. Finally, they should be thanked for their time and their involvement in the session.

Often, PLD group sessions take place within the constraints of an education institution's timetable. A 45-minute or one-hour 'slot' must be optimized by the youth support worker who is mindful of how quickly time passes (once young people have arrived and settled down ready to work), but it also has to be well managed to ensure that personal learning and development is achieved. Furthermore, in order to ensure that the structure is coherent and well managed, it is helpful for youth support workers to prepare, and have to hand, a session plan.

Producing a session plan

There is a plethora of different formats and tools for recording a session plan. Youth support workers will develop a system that meets their own needs. For example, some practitioners (particularly when they are new to the role) may want a very detailed session plan to hand during the session that they can refer to throughout, while more experienced practitioners will simply record key points, timings and activities to act as a prompt. The session plan included here provides an example of the type of document that may be helpful for youth support workers to use (see Figure 6.1).

SESSION PLAN PROFORMA
FOCUS/TOPIC: *This will include a brief description of the topic to be addressed*
LOCATION: *Where will the session take place?*
TIMING: *What time will the session take place and how long will it last?*
GROUP DETAILS: *Group numbers, age, gender, additional needs*
AIM: *The identified aim or 'title' of the session*
OBJECTIVES: *The session objectives; for example, 'participants have the opportunity to...' (PHOTO)*
RESOURCES: *Requirements for the session; for example, pens, paper, flip-chart, case studies, quiz, role play cards, and so on*
STRUCTURE OF SESSION ACTIVITIES AND TIMINGS: *The detail (specific timings and activities), which provides a full overview and plan of the session and can be referred to and followed with ease. For example:*
STAGE ONE
9.30–9.40 Introduction to the session and ice-breaker activity
9.40–9.50 Introduce the topic (aims and objectives on the flip-chart) and check out groups' understanding, and so on....

Figure 6.1 Format for a session plan

This session plan format enables the youth support workers to record all aspects of their planning in detail. They are prompted to set an aim and objectives for the session, they are reminded that they will need to prepare resources in advance and they are provided with a detailed, staged plan (with timings) that can be followed during the session.

Let us return now to Lloyd, Ashraf, Crystal, Jatinder and Sam to see how their planning is progressing. Each youth support worker in Manor Way School has access to the session plan format we have examined. Let us see how the document has been used in each case.

Lloyd is planning a session for eight 15-year-olds, which will last for 45 minutes. Here is his completed session plan:

SESSION PLAN PROFORMA

FOCUS/TOPIC: Session 1 – Self-awareness and goal setting (three sessions in total)

LOCATION: Room G14 Manor Way School

TIMING: 3.30–4.30 (After school)

GROUP DETAILS: Eight 15-year-olds. Five young men, three young women

AIM: Session 1 – How to organize my life: setting priorities for the next year

OBJECTIVES:

- Describe three things in their school life that they enjoy and feel good about, and three goals in relation to education that they would like to achieve in the next year
- List the barriers to achieving their goals
- Identify strategies for overcoming the barriers to achieving their goals
- Write an individual action plan for the next month.

RESOURCES: paper for eight students, eight pens, flip-chart paper and pens, action plan proforma

STRUCTURE OF SESSION, ACTIVITIES AND TIMINGS:

STAGE ONE
3.30–3.40 Introduce myself and the purpose (aim) of the session(s). Individual group members in turn to say how they feel about attending the session(s) and what they hope to get out of it. Note the expectations on the flip-chart. Summarize what this session will cover and how it links to subsequent sessions

3.40–3.45 Agree and write up a contract (ground rules) for the group for the three sessions we will be working together

STAGE TWO
3.45–3.50 Activity:

- Individually, compile a list of aspects of their school life that they feel good about and enjoy. (1 min)
- Share these with a partner and, following discussion, agree the three most important. (4 mins)

3.50–3.55 Having established 'where they are now' in relation to what they are enjoying and are good at in their school life, facilitate group discussion about the range of goals relating to education that young people of their age could achieve. Write these up on the flip-chart

3.55–4.00 Activity:

- Back to pairs to each agree their own three goals for the next year

4.00–4.10 Explain to group that there are likely to be barriers to achievement, get ideas from group about what these might be and list on flip-chart

Activity:

- In same small groups, choose two barriers from the list and agree possible strategies for overcoming them. Present these ideas back to the other group. (Note: the way that these ideas are presented back can be creative and can involve role play, art, music, and other presentation skills)

STAGE THREE
4.10–4.15 Summarize the session so far and make links between the barriers they have identified, the strategies for overcoming the barriers and how these might be applied to their own personal goals

Activity:
Return to the partners that they were working with, discuss possible action steps for the next month (relating to their three key goals). Individually, complete a simple action plan proforma, setting out action steps for the next month. Summarize, remind the group about the next session, thanks and end.

Questions

How well structured do you think this session is?

What concerns do you have (if any) about content and timings?

Having completed the session plan in full, Lloyd is still concerned that he is attempting to fit too much into the session. He is pleased that his structure links clearly with the three-stage model and he is confident that the session flows smoothly and he has thought through each stage of the process. He now has to reconsider and decide what aspect of the session he will change or leave out.

Question

If you were Lloyd, how would you adapt the plan to ensure that the objectives are met, the group work remains structured and the content is manageable in a 45-minute session?

On reflection, Lloyd decides that he will limit the activity planned in stage two from 4.00–4.10 and instead of asking each group to examine two barriers, they will focus on one. He is aware that the session remains 'action-packed', but he thinks that it is important to keep it forward moving and purposeful with plenty of variety in order to accommodate the different learning styles within the group.

Ashraf, like Lloyd, has also completed a detailed session plan for his one-hour PLD group work with a class of 13-year-olds.

SESSION PLAN PROFORMA

FOCUS/TOPIC: Sources of support and how to access them

LOCATION: Room F12 Manor Way School

TIMING: 11.00–12.00

GROUP DETAILS: Class 9WY (28 young people, age 13)

AIM: Who can I go to when I need help?

OBJECTIVES:

- Describe the support that might be needed in relation to education, social and personal development
- List individuals and agencies who can offer support
- Identify how to recognize the support that you need
- Set out how to access the support that is available

RESOURCES: paper and pens for 28 students, flip-chart paper and pens, leaflets/resources on organizations offering support, computer room for internet access for students, prepared case studies

STRUCTURE OF SESSION, ACTIVITIES AND TIMINGS:

STAGE ONE

11.00–11.10 Introduce myself and the aim of the session. Ask individuals to share with a partner an occasion where they have asked for help/support. Brief feedback. Link this to the session aim. Explain what the session will include and agree a contract for working together (on flip-chart)

STAGE TWO

11.10–11.15 In six small groups, work on case studies (one per group) and identify the support needs of the individual concerned

11.15–11.45 In same small groups to research the support available that will meet the needs of the case study. Each group to feedback their case study and sources of support to the whole class

STAGE THREE

11.45–11.50 In pairs, think of an example in your own life when you needed support. How did you know? How do you recognize when you need support yourself? Invite general feedback

11.50–12.00 Summarize activities so far and lead into a whole group discussion on how support can be accessed. Finally, ask individuals to imagine they have a crystal ball, and share with a partner what support needs they may have in the next year. Identify who they might go to for help

End

As Ashraf began to plan the structure of the session, he became aware from his original analysis of appropriate activities (see Chapter 5) that there was little in the way of action planning (stage three) for the participants to undertake. He has decided to 'add in' a final activity whereby individuals reflect on the support needs they may have in the near future and plan who to approach for help.

Ashraf has taken a slightly less detailed approach to completing the session plan than Lloyd; however, he is confident that he has all the information he needs to ensure that the session is structured and will run smoothly.

Crystal is also structuring her PLD session in detail.

SESSION PLAN PROFORMA
FOCUS/TOPIC: Decision making in relation to HE
LOCATION: Careers room Manor Way School
TIMING: Lunch-time session (12.30–1.30)
GROUP DETAILS: Six invited (three male three female) age 17
AIM: What impact my subject choices might have on future decisions about my life?

OBJECTIVES:

- List their own preferred subject area
- Select their own preferred job family
- Describe any job families where they may experience barriers if they choose their preferred subject area
- Write down three action steps to take to research their ideas further

---

RESOURCES: paper and pens for six students, lap-top computer for presentation
STRUCTURE OF SESSION, ACTIVITIES AND TIMINGS:

STAGE ONE
12.30–12.40 Introduce myself and the aim of the session. Ask individuals to share their ideas about their preferred subject of choice for HE

STAGE TWO
12.40–1.00 Computer presentation on job families (note: make links between job families and HE subject areas)

STAGE THREE
1.00–1.15 In pairs, discuss and agree three action steps to take in order to research ideas
1.15–1.30 Ask individuals to share their ideas with the group
General discussion
End

In Chapter 5, we were concerned that Crystal had not attended to a number of concepts underpinning personal learning and development when she designed the activities for her session. Scant attention was paid to learning theory and learning styles and the session objectives were not met by the activities. Now that Crystal has structured the session in more detail, she can see that there is little opportunity for students' interaction and that she is 'dominating' the session. She is aware that this will have a limited impact on the achievement of the objectives.

Questions

What do you feel is missing from the structure of the session?

How would you advise Crystal to structure the session more effectively?

Crystal decides some revision is necessary to her session and she considers limiting her own presentation, and asking the group to research and present back their own ideas about job families and subject areas. She decides to take a more 'facilitative' and less 'presenting' role in the group and will include agreement of a group contract. She will also add a final activity whereby group members discuss their action steps with a partner and write these down. With these amendments made, the session should meet the principles of PLD group work and will be structured in a clear and helpful way.

In the previous chapter, we learned that Jatinder had no time available to plan her session with four pregnant young women in any detail. She had identified an aim, but no objectives were established and no activities planned. She decided to engage in a group discussion and 'play things by ear'. As a result, it is likely that the group work will lack structure. This lack of structure may also mean that Jatinder finds it difficult to manage time and that the session may over or under-run. This could result in the group becoming unfocused and distracted and might lead to individual disengagement or even challenging behaviour (this is discussed further in Chapter 9).

Finally, Sam, the youth worker, is preparing a one-hour PLD session for a group of 14- to 16-year-old young men. So far you have engaged with this process by identifying an aim, objectives and activities for this session.

Activity

Using the blank session plan, structure Sam's session in detail.

SESSION PLAN PROFORMA
FOCUS/TOPIC: LOCATION:
TIMING:
GROUP DETAILS:
AIM:
OBJECTIVES:
RESOURCES:
STRUCTURE OF SESSION, ACTIVITIES AND TIMINGS:

Summary

The importance of structuring a session should not be underestimated. The effectiveness of structure in group work depends on the ability of the facilitator to be aware of, and able to respond to the needs of the group as appropriate. Doel states that:

> It is not so much the degree of structure as its flexibility that is important. All groups benefit from preparation, and almost all of these are helped by a programme of sorts. The extent to which group workers are able to improvise when necessary is of more importance than the degree of structure *per se*. Inexperienced group workers are likely to stick hard and fast or drift aimlessly in roughly equal measure.
>
> (Doel, 2006:50)

The argument for flexibility is a strong one. But it is important not to confuse flexibility with lack of purpose. The three-stage model for structuring group work, introduced in this chapter, does not set out to place a straight-jacket around PLD sessions. Rather, it provides youth support workers with a clear progression in relation to an identified topic, with stated objectives, achieved by undertaking relevant and appropriate activities. Flexibility within this structure is important. For example, the need to respond to individuals who require more support is paramount, as is the ability to extend activities for those who work through them with ease. In addition, there may be areas related to the topic that the group would like to explore in more detail, which the youth support worker has not considered at the planning stage. The three-stage model allows for this flexibility and the youth support worker should feel confident using appropriate skills and techniques, thus enabling them to respond flexibly throughout the session.

Questions

The following questions will assist reflection on the key themes addressed in this chapter:

1 What is the purpose of establishing a structure for PLD sessions?

2 What should happen at each of the three stages in PLD sessions to ensure that they remain purposeful and work towards positive outcomes?

3 Reflect on the last PLD session you undertook, how structured was the session and how, if at all, might you amend the structure in future?

7

Skills to facilitate personal learning and development

Learning Objectives

- Identify a range of techniques and skills for effective facilitation
- Describe the significant features of key facilitation techniques and skills
- Reflect on and develop your own facilitation techniques and skills

Introduction

The planning of PLD sessions has been explored in detail in Chapters 3, 4, 5 and 6. The youth support worker should now feel confident that they have done everything possible in the planning stage to ensure that the session will be a success. By following the FAAST model, the practitioner has established the **Focus** for the session, they have set an **Aim** and appropriate **Activities** for the participants to undertake during the session. In addition, they have **Structured** the group work, using a session plan as a prompt. The point at which the youth support worker and the young people meet together for the PLD session has arrived and it is now the responsibility of the practitioner to utilize a range of **Techniques** and skills to ensure that the session runs smoothly, activities are managed well and optimum personal learning and development is achieved. The role of the youth support worker (explored in detail in Chapter 1) is to facilitate (rather than 'teach' or 'present') the PLD session, drawing on the skills and techniques that they have developed in their one-to-one support work with young people and applying these in a different, but related context.

This chapter begins by setting out a range of techniques that facilitators of PLD sessions will use. It describes the techniques and skills and considers their impact in PLD group sessions. It examines how the techniques and skills are applied in practice, drawing on the case study examples from previous chapters. Throughout, you are invited to reflect on your own use of skills in facilitating group sessions. An activity will be suggested at the end of the chapter to enable you to develop techniques that are central to assisting young people to engage in PLD.

What is effective facilitation?

Chapter 1 established the difference between PLD group work and other activities that take place with groups of young people in education. PLD sessions set out to achieve something different to 'teaching', 'informal education' or 'therapeutic' group work. The learning in PLD sessions is focused on the needs of the individual participants and the young people in the group are given the opportunity to reflect on and plan their own action in relation to the topic under discussion. The role of the youth support worker, therefore, is to 'facilitate' this learning.

Geldard and Geldard explain that facilitation includes a number of components:

> Effective facilitation creates an atmosphere of safety and containment so that children become free to explore, express themselves and gain from the experience. Facilitation involves giving directions and instructions, introducing and organising activities, facilitating discussions, giving support.
>
> (Geldard and Geldard, 2001:127)

For facilitation to be effective, and for the group members to 'become free to explore, express themselves and gain from the experience', it is important that an atmosphere is created that is positive, non-judgemental, open and empathetic to the individuals within the group. The youth support worker will be familiar with these attitudes as they are likely to have been introduced to the 'core conditions' of the person-centred approach (Rogers, 1965) when undertaking training for their one-to-one work with young people. These conditions were examined in Chapter 2, where the principles of student-centred learning were established. The three core conditions are:

- Empathy – trying to understand the lives of the young people with whom the youth support worker is engaging, but from *the young person's* frame of reference.
- Congruence – remaining *genuine* and *real* throughout the session.
- Unconditional positive regard – demonstrating a *non-judgemental approach* to the group members.

Of course, understanding these concepts in theory and applying them in practice is not always straightforward. However, these core conditions form the basis of youth support work and practitioners will understand that they are not a 'cloak' to be put on and taken off as necessary when working with young people, but rather a set of principles that are integrated into professional practice.

Effective facilitation requires the youth support worker to adhere to and, importantly, to *demonstrate* the core conditions in their PLD sessions. This means developing an approach that is alert, sensitive, and engaging, while at the same time being able and prepared to challenge attitudes and behaviour, and support any individual in the group who, for whatever reason, feels vulnerable. Group members should feel that the facilitator cares and responds in a way that is not confrontational, sarcastic or demeaning. By so doing, a relationship of trust will form, and it is in these conditions of mutual respect that young people will be encouraged to take responsibility for their personal learning and development. In practical terms, this means listening to the young people, encouraging participation and discussion, sharing ideas and experiences, providing new experiences on which the group members can reflect and from which they can learn and, importantly, using humour thoughtfully and appropriately in the session. It also means being prepared to challenge behaviour, language, values and assumptions where necessary without jeopardizing the positive working relationship with the group. To sum up, be human with the group, be real, be yourself.

Egan (1973) identifies five functions of facilitation as applied to group work. In brief, these functions are:

- setting 'goals' (aims and objectives) for the session;
- using knowledge and experience to foster a climate conducive to learning;
- behaving in a way that encourages group members to adopt an attitude of respect with their peers;
- ensuring that the group stays focused on the topic;
- facilitating rather than leading the group.

Although Egan focuses on facilitation in *therapeutic* group settings, it is clear that these functions can equally be adapted to PLD group work, with particular emphasis placed on managing the group by modelling a student-centred and empathic 'way of being' while working towards guardianship, rather than leadership. Bentley explains:

> Facilitation is the provision of opportunities, resources, encouragement and support for the group to succeed in achieving its objectives, and to do this through enabling the group to take control and responsibility for the way they proceed.
>
> (Bentley, 1994: 31)

To summarize, effective facilitation of PLD group work requires the following:

- regard for a student-centred and experiential approach to learning;
- adherence to the core conditions of empathy, congruence and unconditional positive regard;
- application of a range of techniques and skills to encourage participation, engagement and reflection in learning;
- challenging the group, or individuals when necessary;
- awareness of and response to the group dynamic (discussed fully in Chapter 8);
- flexibility (based on effective planning and structuring of the session);
- humour.

Having determined the role of the facilitator and identified an approach to facilitation that will enable PLD to take place, the next step is to examine the key techniques and skills necessary to facilitate PLD group work with young people.

Key facilitation techniques and skills

There are a number of texts that offer helpful insights into skills for group sessions with young people (Geldard and Geldard, 2001; Malekoff, 2004; Doel, 2006). However, a guide to facilitating PLD group sessions for youth support workers would not be taking its topic seriously if it did not explore how key techniques and skills are used in practice to encourage personal learning and development. The following techniques and skills are examined in this chapter:

- active listening and responding;
- helpful questioning;
- summarizing;
- information sharing;
- challenging;
- immediacy.

A brief analysis of each will follow. In order to reflect on how the skills are applied in practice, we return to our youth support worker case studies introduced in previous chapters to see examples of the skills being used.

Activity

As you are reading about these facilitation techniques and skills, visualize yourself in your own group sessions.

How effectively do you use these techniques and skills?

Which do you do well?

Which could you develop?

Active listening and responding

Listening actively and responding appropriately are central to the effectiveness of group work. This requires youth support workers to engage all their senses, not just their hearing, in order to 'pick up' the key messages (spoken and unspoken) within the group. The skills of active listening and responding will be familiar to youth support workers as they are central to their one-to-one work with clients. However, there is a difference between focusing on and listening to an individual in a one-to-one intervention, and listening to a young person (or more than one young person) who is speaking during a group session. As well as listening and responding to individual voices (and non-verbal clues), the youth support worker must also be sensitive to what the group as an entity is 'saying'.

Active listening requires the following:

- Hearing the words that are being said, the language chosen, the tone of voice, the volume.
- Observing the way that the words are spoken, the facial expressions, the gestures that accompany the words.
- 'Sensing' the feelings behind the words, the confidence of the speaker, the level of bravado/vulnerability.
- Assessing the purpose of the words, to share, enhance, take a risk, confront, disrupt or damage.
- Remaining alert to the group's response to individual contributions and your own interventions. Is the group engaged? Does the group understand? Is the group aware of how the topic is relevant to them? How do you know, what clues are you picking up?
- Evaluating the impact of sub-groups and power dynamics within the group. Is there a dominant 'faction' or individual and a silent majority, for example?

Responding appropriately requires the following:

- Demonstrating that you are listening actively by engaging eye contact with the speaker, while at the same time remaining alert to the responses of others.
- Ensuring that throughout the session, eye contact is maintained with all group members (in a large group it can be helpful to visualize three of four 'sections' in the room and make eye contact with each in turn to avoid the trap of engaging only with a small number of participants in one part of the room).
- Making encouraging para-verbal responses (umm, aah, OK) to demonstrate your continued interest.
- Reflecting back key words to emphasize meaning.
- Taking immediate action if what you are listening to (either from an individual or within the group) requires you to do so.

In the following case study, Lloyd, who is working with a group of eight 15-year-olds, demonstrates his ability to listen actively and to respond appropriately to an individual group member *and* to the group as an entity.

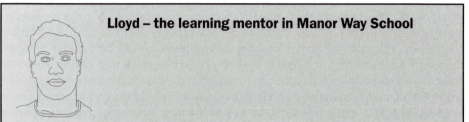

Lloyd – the learning mentor in Manor Way School

Lloyd has been asked to plan three sessions that will take place after school for a group of young people who have been truanting. He has set an aim and objectives for each session, planned activities and devised a session plan that sets out a clear structure for session one. Lloyd is meeting with the group for the first time. He has introduced himself and has asked each of the group members to introduce themselves and to say how they feel about attending and what they hope to get out of the session/s.

Natasha: (avoiding eye contact, arms folded, slumped in the chair) I'm Natasha. I feel angry about being here. I don't understand why we have to come to these sessions. Why couldn't we just have got one detention? We all know we were truanting. We got caught. Let's just have the punishment and get it over with. I don't see the point of being here for three weeks. It's not fair.

Lloyd: Thanks Natasha for being so honest. It's really good that you can share how you feel. Looking around the group, I can see that you're not alone in being upset and frustrated and I can understand why you might be feeling that way. It's important that we are all comfortable within this group to say how we feel. But . . . I also asked you to say what you hoped to get out of these sessions. See if you can 'put aside' your angry feelings for a minute, and imagine that you want to be here. If you wanted to be here, what would you want to get out of this session?

Lloyd is showing that he has assessed accurately how Natasha is feeling and he is also demonstrating empathy for her situation. In his response, Lloyd conveys that he has sensed similar feelings from other group members (by being aware of the body language, with other participants sitting slumped in their chairs, avoiding his eye contact and by sensing a tangible atmosphere of negativity, hostility and resistance in the room). Lloyd recognizes the feelings but neither colludes with them nor challenges them. Already he is showing that he takes the group seriously. Over time, this genuine (congruent) response will help the participants to build a relationship of trust with Lloyd. They know that he listens to and understands their feelings, and is not 'frightened off' by their negativity.

Listening and responding are at the very heart of any group interaction. Group members listen to themselves, each other and the facilitator, and therefore every response that the facilitator makes will send out a message that is processed by each member of the group. A failure to listen and respond appropriately can be extremely damaging. Group members may feel:

- ignored;
- unsupported;
- misunderstood;
- worthless;
- not taken seriously.

If this continues, participants may be unwilling to make contributions, are likely to disengage, and any credibility and respect for the youth support worker is jeopardized.

The remaining facilitation skills are linked inextricably to listening and responding appropriately.

Helpful questioning

It is important, first, to establish that the key reason for asking questions in PLD group sessions is not for the facilitator to find out information about the participants and their lives; rather, it is to encourage the participants themselves to reflect on and be curious about how they think and feel about issues. It is through this reflection (or deeper thinking) that insight and learning can be achieved. There are a number of different types of question, some more helpful than others in generating reflection and thought. These include:

- Open questions – what? when? how? and why? (or the less threatening 'I wonder why?') invite a response that is more than simply yes or no. To that end, they are extremely helpful in encouraging young people to explore their ideas in depth

- Closed questions – did you? will you? can you? have you? invite a yes, no, or don't know response. This is likely to close any interaction down, and does not encourage reflection. However, at times a closed question can be useful to establish facts, as long as it is followed up by an open question. For example, 'do you know what I mean by self-awareness?' (closed) 'what do you think it means?' (open)

- Hypothetical questions – imagine that . . ., what if? pose a potential scenario about which young people reflect. For example 'Imagine that you see someone in the school bullying another pupil. What would you do?' By setting up a hypothetical situation and placing themselves in it, young people can examine their own thoughts, feelings and responses and are encouraged to develop or even change their thinking as the consequences of their reactions become clear.

- Clarifying questions – I think you are saying this . . . have I got it right? Sometimes a supplementary or 'clarifying' question needs to be asked to ensure understanding.

- Leading questions – you wouldn't want to do that, would you? are based on value judgements. The facilitator's! These are never helpful as they may not be accurate. It can be difficult for group members to openly disagree with what the facilitator has said.

- Multiple questions – have you talked about this before, when, what did you say? Asking more than one question at a time can be confusing and limiting. It is likely that participants will respond either to the first, or to the last question and therefore the remaining unanswered questions will have to be reframed or repeated.

Let us return to Ashraf who is working with a class-sized group of 13-year-olds. Like Lloyd, Ashraf has planned the session fully and he is engaging the group in a discussion about the topic; how they can access support should they need it.

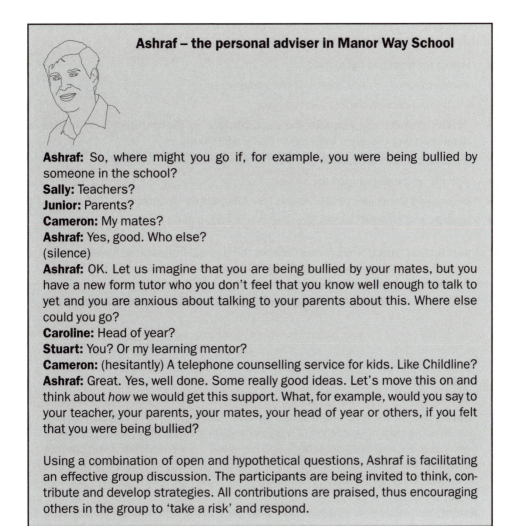

Ashraf – the personal adviser in Manor Way School

Ashraf: So, where might you go if, for example, you were being bullied by someone in the school?
Sally: Teachers?
Junior: Parents?
Cameron: My mates?
Ashraf: Yes, good. Who else?
(silence)
Ashraf: OK. Let us imagine that you are being bullied by your mates, but you have a new form tutor who you don't feel that you know well enough to talk to yet and you are anxious about talking to your parents about this. Where else could you go?
Caroline: Head of year?
Stuart: You? Or my learning mentor?
Cameron: (hesitantly) A telephone counselling service for kids. Like Childline?
Ashraf: Great. Yes, well done. Some really good ideas. Let's move this on and think about *how* we would get this support. What, for example, would you say to your teacher, your parents, your mates, your head of year or others, if you felt that you were being bullied?

Using a combination of open and hypothetical questions, Ashraf is facilitating an effective group discussion. The participants are being invited to think, contribute and develop strategies. All contributions are praised, thus encouraging others in the group to 'take a risk' and respond.

If youth support workers do not take the opportunity to ask helpful questions, they risk the session taking on the features of an interrogation, where closed questions are fired at participants with monotonous regularity. Where this happens, youth support workers are likely to feel that individuals are not cooperating or 'opening up' in the session. In reality, there is little or no encouragement to do so.

Summarizing

The skill of summarizing (sometimes referred to as 'paraphrasing') is helpful (but often underused) in both one-to-one interactions and group work. Unlike active listening and helpful questioning, summarizing is not a skill that is normally utilized in everyday conversation and therefore it requires effort and thought. Put simply, summarizing is 'repeating back' the main points that have been raised. Done well, use of this skill encourages group members to:

- reflect on what has been said;
- ask themselves – is this what I or the group mean?;
- clarify and deepen their understanding;
- develop respect and empathy for the facilitator, as the youth support worker is demonstrating that they have heard and understood;
- make links between themes that have been raised during the session;
- provide 'punctuation' for the session;
- ensure that the stages of the session (see Chapter 6) are linked;
- identify and consolidate the learning that is taking place.

Let us return to Ashraf's session to observe the skill of summarizing being used.

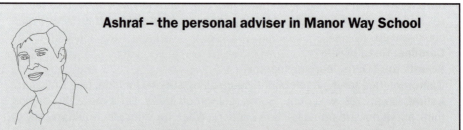

Ashraf – the personal adviser in Manor Way School

Ashraf: OK, so we've thought about who we might go to if we need support. You've come up with some great suggestions for people who can support you, both in school and outside school. Let me think . . . we had teachers, parents or carers, friends, brothers and sisters, youth support workers like me and other specialist agencies. For example?
Katie: Childline.
Ashraf: Yes, excellent. What we have also done is thought about how we would approach and contact these individuals and agencies, and it seems that many of us feel anxious sometimes about doing this. We felt that it might be difficult to find the right words to express the support we need. What did we say about this?
Caroline: That we should think about exactly what we want to say.
Junior: And maybe write it down or go through it with someone else first.
Ashraf: Yes, great. So far we have looked at the kind of support that you have needed in the past and we've also identified people and organizations that can help. But what about the future? How might what's been learned so far have an effect on your lives in the future?

Ashraf is using summarizing skills throughout this interaction. He is not only summarizing the key points himself, but he is also inviting the group to engage in the summary. He uses the skill of summary to link activities that have been undertaken earlier in the session and to move from a 'past' to a 'future'-oriented scenario. Notice, too, how Ashraf's use of language is inclusive. He uses 'we' rather than 'you' placing himself in the group rather than separate from it.

It could be argued that summarizing at frequent intervals might feel repetitive, unnatural or even patronizing. In fact, this could not be further from the truth. The facilitator will *reinforce* rather than *repeat* key points that have been made. The process will feel natural and comfortable within the interaction, learning is 'captured' before moving on and group members will feel listened to, rather than patronized.

Information sharing

It is likely that in every PLD session, at some point, information will be shared. Youth support workers (again, from their one-to-one support work with young people) will be aware of the significance of the choice of words here. Information *sharing* is not the same as information *giving*. It is important to recognize, particularly when working with a group of young people, that information relevant to the topic will already be held by individuals within the group. Information that young people share with each other is likely to have more credibility and feel more relevant than that provided by the facilitator, so it is the role of the facilitator to encourage group members themselves to share information. Of course, by so doing the youth support worker will be able to identify any 'gaps' or inaccuracies in the information being shared and can respond to these appropriately. Sharing information requires the facilitator to do the following:

- Obtain accurate information, relevant to the topic before the session starts.
- Gather together information sources and resources that can be used in the session.
- Check what information the group has about the topic already.
- Structure activities that enable participants to research/share information with each other.
- Present information in an accessible and easily understood form (i.e. ensure that the language/visuals are clear, accurate and free from stereotyping, bias or jargon).
- Be aware of the 'pace' with which information is shared – keep it clear, provide 'bite-sized chunks' rather than a feast, and ask the group to summarize what they have heard/seen in order to check understanding.
- Back up spoken information with written/visual information (e.g. handouts/leaflets) where appropriate.

In Chapter 6, Crystal, the careers adviser, planned a lunch-time session on decision making in relation to higher education. The session is for six young people, 17 years of age, who are considering progressing to higher education after school. Initially,

Crystal had chosen to provide a visual presentation, but on reflection (and mindful of the principles of PLD group work) Crystal amended her plans to include a more interactive approach to sharing information. In the following extract Crystal is encouraging group members to make the link between occupational choices and subject choices in higher education.

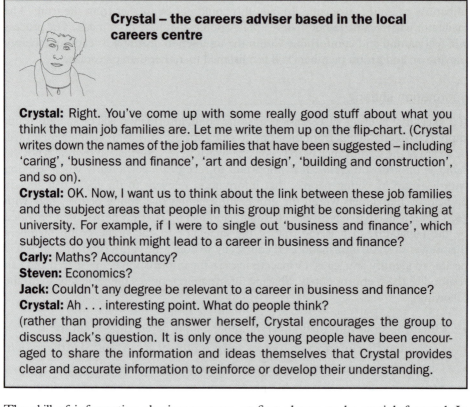

Crystal – the careers adviser based in the local careers centre

Crystal: Right. You've come up with some really good stuff about what you think the main job families are. Let me write them up on the flip-chart. (Crystal writes down the names of the job families that have been suggested – including 'caring', 'business and finance', 'art and design', 'building and construction', and so on).

Crystal: OK. Now, I want us to think about the link between these job families and the subject areas that people in this group might be considering taking at university. For example, if I were to single out 'business and finance', which subjects do you think might lead to a career in business and finance?

Carly: Maths? Accountancy?

Steven: Economics?

Jack: Couldn't any degree be relevant to a career in business and finance?

Crystal: Ah . . . interesting point. What do people think?

(rather than providing the answer herself, Crystal encourages the group to discuss Jack's question. It is only once the young people have been encouraged to share the information and ideas themselves that Crystal provides clear and accurate information to reinforce or develop their understanding.

The skill of information sharing appears, at first glance, to be straightforward. In reality, it is an advanced skill. Sometimes, as professionals, we are so keen to share valuable knowledge and information that we risk overloading or bombarding young people with 'pearls of wisdom' that are neither relevant nor useful to them. Reid and Fielding advise caution:

> We must be careful not to bombard or deluge young people with information. When this happens the information we give is often inappropriate, and although it may make us feel secure it rarely meets the young person's needs.
>
> (Reid and Fielding, 2007: 78)

It is crucial to find a balance between this and the equally unhelpful response 'I'm not going to tell you – you need to find it out for yourself!'. Youth support workers should be mindful of striking a balance between the two: finding out what the young people know already; establishing what they need to know at this stage; and planning interesting activities and input to help them to 'fill the gaps'.

Challenging

The first point relating to the skill of challenge that should be established is that 'challenging' should be a positive and supportive experience that enhances learning within the group. A challenge is *not* a confrontation, disagreement or stand-off between facilitator and group member/s. Rather, it is an intervention that should be used sensitively within the ethos of student-centred learning, while adhering to the core conditions. Challenging should be used at the following times:

- To attend to discrepancies or inaccuracies in what group members are saying.
- To encourage individuals to consider the consequences of their actions.
- To address discriminatory language or inappropriate behaviour.
- To help young people to gain new perspectives and be realistic about what they can achieve.
- To respond if the group contract (ground rules) have been broken.

Challenging is not a single skill. In order to challenge effectively, youth support workers will draw on a range of techniques (already discussed in this chapter) and use them appropriately depending on the reason for the challenge. For example, in relation to the points listed above, challenges could be made in the following ways:

- *Discrepancies or inaccuracies:* the skills of questioning and information sharing can help to challenge any discrepancies or inaccuracies in what individuals are saying. Rather than say 'that is not correct', or, worse 'you've got that wrong', the youth support worker might ask 'what do other people think?' or 'does anyone have a different view?' or 'let us have a look and see what information we can find out about this that will clarify the situation'.

- *Encouraging individuals to think about the consequences of their actions:* again, questioning skills and in particular hypothetical questions can be valuable when considering consequences. Questions such as 'what if we go ahead and make the decision to leave home, what might it be like?' or 'let's imagine that we carry on being disruptive in class and that we keep on getting excluded. What do we think will end up happening?' Using hypothetical questions encourages reflection, raising awareness of the possible consequences of particular actions. The alternative (telling group members that something is not a good idea, or that they should not do it) is neither student-centred, nor likely to be listened to.

- *Addressing discriminatory behaviour or language:* (managing challenging behaviour is discussed fully in Chapter 9). In brief, it is critical that discriminatory language and inappropriate or bullying behaviour are challenged immediately. The facilitator may need to adjust their facilitative approach in order to ensure that individuals in the group are made aware that their behaviour or language is unacceptable. It is critical to base the challenge on the *language* or the *behaviour* and not the *person*; for example, 'that kind of language is not appropriate in this session and we need to make sure that it stops now', or 'nobody in this room should feel bullied by anyone else. That behaviour is unhelpful and will stop now'. It can be useful to return to the group contract (ground rules) established at the start of the session; for example, 'we agreed that we would treat each other with respect and I've just heard something that breaks that rule. Let's remind ourselves about what treating each other with respect means so that we can make sure that the contract isn't broken again'. Although the challenge must be clear and direct, it should avoid being confrontational or aggressive, thus risking breaking down the relationship of trust with the group.

- *Gaining new perspectives and encouraging realism:* again, the use of hypothetical questions can be very effective in encouraging group members to be realistic. For example, 'OK, you are saying that carrying a gun with you when you go out with your mates might make you feel safe. Let's think for a minute about how and when the gun might be used and what might be the consequences'. Or 'you are saying to me that when you get angry in class, you swear at your teacher, and run out. What other options can people think of instead of running out of the room?'
- *Breaking the ground rules:* by writing down the agreed ground rules at the start of the session, the youth support worker has a great resource at their disposal. Pointing at the contract (if, for example the contract specifies 'mobile phones on silent' and a phone can be heard), and raising an eyebrow, can be enough to challenge the group member concerned. Or, a simple reminder 'what did we say about mobile phones?' can draw attention to and challenge the group member concerned without humiliating or confronting them.

Immediacy

The skill of immediacy is closely allied to the skill of challenging. Immediacy happens when the youth support worker interrupts the 'flow' of the interaction to deal with the 'here and now' in the group. The youth support worker will rely on their active listening skills and their intuition and insight in order to know when the use of immediacy is appropriate. The skill of immediacy is useful in the following situations:

- *When the group appears to be disengaged, distracted, overexcited or unfocused:* by saying, 'there seems to be something going on here that is getting in the way of us working together in this session. What do we need to do about it?' The youth support worker directly addresses the group rather than continues to introduce yet another activity in the hope that participants will be motivated to take part.
- *If there is a strong emotional undercurrent:* sometimes young people may become angry or upset in sessions (as might the youth support worker). Again, rather than continue the session and pretend that all is well, the youth support worker should acknowledge the feelings and deal with them in a way that keeps the group members safe. For example, 'I get the feeling that some people in this group feel really angry about what I've just said. I wonder why?' or 'am I the only one who felt sad when we watched that film clip? Let's talk about how it made us feel'.
- *When an immediate response is required:* young people will react positively to praise. If a good piece of work has been observed it should be acknowledged as

such. For example, 'hold on, before we carry on with this, I want to say how impressed I am by the way in which you have discussed this difficult subject'.

Immediacy should always be used tentatively. Using statements such as 'I get the feeling that . . .' or 'I could be wrong here, but . . .,' or 'is it just me or do others feel . . .' allows young people to think, reflect and agree or disagree. Immediacy serves to open up a dialogue with the group and demonstrate that the facilitator is engaging fully with the session on an emotional level.

Let us return to Jatinder who uses both challenge and immediacy in her group session for four pregnant young women in school. You will remember that Jatinder ran out of time to prepare her session in any detail (see Chapter 6). The session topic is healthy eating and exercise in pregnancy, and features a group discussion as the only activity.

Jatinder – personal adviser (working with teenage pregnancy issues) in Manor Way School

Jatinder: What do we think about eating healthily in pregnancy? How important is it?

Sarah: I don't think it is. I'm just looking forward to eating for two and stuffing my face with tons of sweets.

(everyone laughs)

Jatinder: OK, that's one approach. But what might happen if Sarah does that?

(no response)

Jatinder: Well, let's imagine that Sarah eats her way through her pregnancy and puts on loads of weight. What might be the consequences for her and for the baby?

Emma: She'll have to lose it all again or she won't get into her clothes.

(everyone laughs)

Jatinder: That's true! But what about her health and her baby's health too?

(no response. Group members shrug their shoulders and avoid eye contact. Sarah starts to nudge Emma and giggle)

Jatinder: We started off this session with a really good discussion didn't we? But I'm feeling that we are losing a bit of concentration now and getting distracted. Have I got that right?

(silence)

Jatinder: What do people think?

Sarah: It was all right to start with. But we're a bit fed up with just chatting about stuff. We thought that we might be able to do things when we come for these sessions, not just sit around and talk. It's a bit boring to be honest.

(the others nod and giggle)

This example demonstrates that Jatinder can use challenge and immediacy effectively. What it also shows is that she is paying the price for her lack of preparation. The participants are becoming bored with their elongated group discussion and require additional activities to build on and enhance their learning. However, by using the skill of immediacy, the group have been able to air their views and Jatinder can make changes to the session as appropriate.

Summary

The role of the facilitator requires the development of a range of techniques and skills, which are also central to the work of youth support practitioners in their one-to-one relationships with young people. But, the ways in which the skills are adapted for use in the group context is critical. Some of these techniques have been examined in this chapter, and demonstrated 'in practice' through the case study examples.

Finally, to help you to reflect on your own skills in group work, the following activity provides you with the opportunity to undertake a 'skills audit', identifying the skills you use in group sessions, your strengths and areas for development.

Activity

Reflect on a piece of group work you have undertaken recently and complete the skills inventory in Table 7.1.

Table 7.1 Skills inventory

SKILL	Examples of how/when I use the skill in group sessions	How did use of the skill demonstrate the core conditions of empathy, congruence and unconditional positive regard?	Strengths in relation to this skill	Areas for development in relation to this skill	Action to take to develop this skill for group work
Active listening and responding					
Helpful questioning					
Summarizing					
Information sharing					
Challenge					
Immediacy					

8

Group dynamics

Learning Objectives

· Identify and describe a range of theories and concepts related to group dynamics
· Evaluate the effect of group dynamics in PLD group sessions
· Analyse the impact of group dynamics theory on practice

Introduction

Throughout this book, parallels have been drawn between the one-to-one helping relationships that youth support workers engage in with young people, and PLD group sessions. For example, PLD group work aims for the same outcomes as one-to-one work (informed decision making and positive change), interactions are structured in a similar way (a three-stage model that suggests a purposeful progression) and the skills that youth support workers use in both contexts are the same, but are adapted for purpose. Although these parallels exist, there are key differences between a one-to-one supportive relationship and a group interaction. The main difference, of course, is the group itself. Therefore, a book about personal learning and development in groups has a responsibility to address the concept of group dynamics, and examine the impact of group processes on the learning and development of its members. Groups are complex. They are composed of a number of individuals, each with unique qualities, skills, personalities, experiences, expectations, insights and needs. Add in the role of the facilitator, their own expectations, plans, hopes and fears, and the 'mix' becomes even more complex. Not only should the facilitator be able to empathize with, value and respect the rights of each individual within the group, but they should also be mindful of the need to pay attention to the entity that is 'the group' itself. In other words, the group will develop a set of characteristics, norms and behaviours all of its own.

An added complication, when examining group dynamics in youth support practice, is that the roles of youth support workers vary and therefore the context in which

PLD group work takes place is likely to be quite different from one practitioner to the next. In Chapter 1, the range of roles constituting youth support practice is discussed and attention is drawn to the different contexts in which PLD group work happens. Some youth support workers may be based in schools while others will be visitors to them (or will work in related educational establishments such as Pupil Referral Units). Some youth support workers (e.g. teaching assistants and learning mentors) will have the opportunity to develop a relationship with a group of young people over a period of time, while others (e.g. careers advisers and personal advisers) may be required to deliver 'one-off' sessions. Some youth support professionals (teaching assistants in particular) may find themselves working with small groups within a larger-sized class environment (when the teacher has identified students in the classroom who need more intensive or individual support). The context in which the group takes place will have an influence on the dynamic within the group and the development of the group as an entity (Lewin et al., 1994).

This chapter examines two approaches for understanding group dynamics and considers how knowledge of the theory can inform the planning and delivery of PLD group sessions. It uses case study examples to illustrate group dynamics and processes in action. Although the impact of group dynamics on PLD sessions is discussed in detail, this chapter does not set out to provide suggestions about how these dynamics are managed (this follows in Chapter 9). Instead, it focuses on the theory informing practice as an aid to gaining greater understanding about the ways in which groups and individuals in those groups function. A note of caution should now be sounded. An understanding of the theory of group dynamics is both helpful and relevant to youth support workers, but the urge to 'overinterpret' or 'meddle' with the dynamic of a group can be harmful and should be avoided.

It is important to make clear at this point that the topic of group dynamics (like learning theory, in Chapter 2) is huge. To attempt to condense it into a single chapter without appearing to oversimplify or underestimate its significance is a challenge. What follows offers an introduction to the theory of group dynamics (a further explanation can be found in Johnson and Johnson, 1997).

Group dynamics: the theory

There are a range of theories that have been developed in order to describe and make sense of the ways in which groups form, operate and end. Most notable of these are Bion (1961), Tuckman (1965), Tuckman and Jensen (1977), Hadfield (1992), Belbin (1993), Vernelle (1994), Fatout (1996) and Slavin (1997). Some of these theorists (Fatout, Tuckman) examine group dynamics from a chronological or developmental perspective (from conception to closure), whereby the stage of the group's development is seen as the single most significant factor in influencing the dynamic. Others (Belbin, Bion, Vernelle and Slavin) focus more specifically on the individual behaviours in the group and examine how the 'mix' of individuals influences the emerging dynamic of the group. This dynamic can change significantly, for example, if a particular group member is absent. Both approaches have value; neither are exclusive and both are introduced in this chapter.

Chronological approach

The thinking behind the chronological approach and its impact on group dynamics is that every group progresses through a number of stages, and the particular stage of development will influence the dynamic within it. This approach to understanding group dynamics is especially pertinent for youth support workers who have the opportunity to build and sustain a relationship with a group over a period of time. In Chapters 3–7, we observed a number of youth support workers planning, developing and delivering PLD sessions. Of these, Lloyd, Crystal, Jatinder and Sam are each working with groups for more than one session. They must be mindful of the ways in which their groups are likely to develop and the characteristics and behaviours that may be in evidence at each stage. Ashraf, however, facilitates his group for a 'one-off' session. As a consequence, he does not have the opportunity to witness the influence of the development of the group with regard to group dynamics beyond the one session. In addition Lloyd, Crystal, Jatinder and Sam are working with groups that have been formed specifically for the PLD sessions; they did not previously exist in their own right. Ashraf's group, by contrast, is a class of 13-year-old pupils who have been working together for some time, and therefore a dynamic would already be established (although, of course, Ashraf will make his own impact on this dynamic). So, what are the stages of development that will influence the group dynamic?

Tuckman (1965) describes four stages through which any group will progress. He later added a fifth and final stage to the process. The five stages are:

1   forming;
2   storming;
3   norming;
4   performing;
5   adjourning (mourning).

It is helpful for youth support workers to be aware of the characteristics of each of the five stages, as it is likely that any group with which they are working will exhibit certain traits and behaviours that will be influenced by its chronological development.

The first of these stages, 'forming', is likely to be characterized by an initial uncertainty and nervousness within the group. Group members may feel anxious or even angry about being part of this group; alternatively, they may feel positive, excited and full of anticipation. There will be levels of expectation within the group (high or low) about why they are there and what they will be doing. The aim of the facilitator at this stage is to create a positive working environment that is conducive to PLD taking place. Geldard and Geldard explain:

> During the forming stage group members develop a sense of trust, safety and belonging. Often a group leader can help to create trust by modelling behaviour which illustrates that he or she is prepared to trust the group.
>
> (Geldard and Geldard, 2001: 106)

Building this relationship of trust may take time, and investing in a discussion about what the purpose of the group is, why participants have been selected to be part of it and how it is planned to function, should help in the process. Because PLD sessions are different to other group settings in education (e.g. teaching), the facilitator should ensure that their own expectations of the group are made clear. Often, the forming stage will be characterized by a dependency on the facilitator. The group members will look to the youth support worker for guidance and to make the group feel 'safe'. It is important therefore that the youth support worker does just that, while at the same time encouraging individuals to participate and take responsibility for their learning, thereby becoming fully involved as members of the group. The following example illustrates a group at the forming stage.

Kelly – the teaching assistant in Manor Way School

Kelly has been asked by a form tutor to work with a small group of 15-year-olds on their time management skills. The young people in the group are consistently late for school, they rarely hand work in on time, and they are always the last students to arrive back in the classroom after break. Kelly meets the group for the first of six 30-minute sessions. There are six young people present. To begin with, the students arrive late, they seem uncertain about how to respond to the session and each other. There are a few giggles, some sideways glances, some fidgeting and a general feeling of anticipation. At the same time, Kelly is aware of a negative undercurrent from some group members, picked up by 'listening' to the body language in the room. No one seems willing to participate actively in the session. Although all participants know each other, they do not know each other as a group. Kelly feels a responsibility to generate some energy in the group and to get the participants 'onside'. She resists the urge to challenge their unresponsiveness. Instead, she takes time to make the group feel safe by gently encouraging participation through activities that involve the young people in communicating with other individuals and with the group as a whole. Gradually, the young people begin to 'open up' and participate. Kelly feels that she is negotiating this early 'forming' stage effectively.

The second stage in Tuckman's model is described as 'storming'. Simply put, as the group begins to identify itself as an established entity in its own right, individual responses to being part of the group will emerge. Having encouraged autonomy and ownership at the 'forming' stage, the group members will begin to accept the invitation to take an active part in the sessions. This can result in a 'testing out' phase, where young people may begin to challenge each other, the purpose of the session or the facilitator. Dominant personalities are likely to come to the fore, with self-appointed spokespeople contributing frequently (and not always helpfully) while others in the group appear less involved and more withdrawn. Separate factions may begin to emerge, polarizing the group into two or more sub-groups. The facilitator's skills and ability to keep the group safe will be tested, as the young people seek to 'check out' the parameters that have been set in the sessions.

For the facilitator, this stage of the group process is likely to feel daunting at best and chaotic at worst. Inexperienced youth support workers may question their own group management skills and worry that the group will never 'gel' and work constructively together. The positive working environment that was envisaged by the practitioner at the outset may now feel like an unrealistic and unobtainable goal. However, it is important to recognize that what the group is asking for here is a facilitator who can manage conflict effectively by remaining calm, unflustered, genuine and supportive. On the one hand, the group members are likely to rally against an aggressive or confrontational approach and on the other, they will not respect a facilitator who is passive and unresponsive. Firmness, clarity, congruence and a sense of fair play is what is required of the facilitator at this stage, coupled with the understanding that this is a phase and not a permanent state of being. Let us see how effectively Kelly is able to navigate the storming stage with her group of 15-year-olds.

Kelly – the teaching assistant in Manor Way School

The group have now met together on two occasions. On the third session, Kelly is aware that the group is noisier than previously and seems unfocused. One group member leaps out of his chair, kicks it away and says angrily, 'what's the point of this session? It's a waste of time'. Another group member agrees (although less forcefully) while others in the room start to giggle or look concerned. Another group member says 'stop moaning. It's better being here than going to lessons'. Kelly is aware that she must deal at once with the violent behaviour while at the same time supporting the group and using facilitative rather than disciplinary skills. Because she understands the theory underpinning group processes, she has been expecting some 'storming' behaviour. She remains calm, acknowledges the anger in the group, asks the disruptive member to talk about how he feels and encourages other members of the group to respond. Kelly also returns to the group contract (see Chapter 6), which was completed in the first session to negotiate ground 'rules' to keep all group members safe in the sessions. Kelly continues to facilitate a heated but positive discussion that concludes in agreement that everyone will 'give the group a chance'. Kelly leaves the session feeling relieved that this early 'storming' phase has been adequately navigated.

The third stage in the group process is described by Tuckman as the 'norming' phase. Once the 'storming' stage has been 'worked through' by the group (with the assistance of the facilitator), group members should feel more prepared to engage with the task in hand (namely their personal learning and development). They should also begin to feel that they 'belong' to the group and they should experience a growing sense of ownership of the group process. That is not to say that all is harmonious. Clearly, there will be a range of different personalities in the group; some who prefer to speak out; others who take a less active part, but overall, there should be a sense of tolerance and equilibrium. As the title of this stage suggests, the group 'norms' will be emerging and individuals will begin to feel safe and comfortable in their position within the group.

At this stage, the role of the facilitator should be to take a more cooperative and less directive style. The youth support worker will begin to feel more 'part' of the group and less 'in charge' of and 'responsible' for it. In effect, the power dynamic has shifted and the group members no longer require someone to 'take control' and make the sessions safe – they can do that for themselves. It is now that the group begins to engage with the task in hand. They concentrate more on the topic and the activities that have been planned for them and less on how they should operate as a member of the group. Kelly's sessions on timekeeping are progressing and the dynamic in the group has shifted further as the norming stage is established.

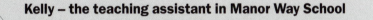

Kelly – the teaching assistant in Manor Way School

In session four Kelly is aware that there has been a change in the demeanour of the group. There is greater cooperation among group members and Kelly capitalizes on this by structuring activities in such a way that those who have not worked together in a pair or a small group in earlier sessions now have the chance to do so. Group members who had previously expressed disinterest are beginning to engage with the subject matter. Kelly notices a greater tolerance among the young people, both for the views and opinions of their fellow group members and for the range of personalities within the group.

Kelly is spending much less time facilitating the group dynamic and much more time facilitating learning about the topic. There is an atmosphere of productivity and humour. Noise levels are high, but not unacceptably so. At the end of the session, Kelly invites the group to think about how they would like to use the next session. What themes would they like to work on in more depth? She is pleased and surprised by the positive response, with suggestions coming from what would have appeared, in earlier sessions, to be the most unlikely sections of the group.

The fourth stage in Tuckman's theory of group processes is the 'performing' stage. By now, the group should be working as an entity with its own established identity. There is likely to be greater cooperation, autonomy and a clear sense of ownership of the group. A closeness or even intimacy may develop at this stage, whereby the group members are likely to take greater risks with the experiences and feelings that they disclose to each other. The role of the facilitator at this stage is to keep the participants focused and 'on task', encouraging and working with their responses while at the same time ensuring that the topic, the aims and the objectives of the session are addressed, and that the activities undertaken optimize learning. The facilitator needs to develop a heightened awareness of any difficult or painful material that may begin to emerge as the group develops trust among its members. Kelly has now reached session five. Has the group achieved the performing stage of its development?

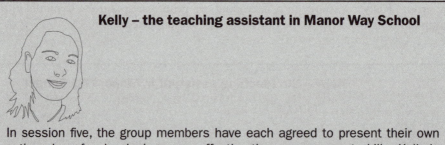

Kelly – the teaching assistant in Manor Way School

In session five, the group members have each agreed to present their own action plans for developing more effective time management skills. Kelly is delighted that every group member with the exception of one person has put together a short presentation, and is able to speak openly to the group about how they intend to improve their time management skills. Kelly does not challenge the one group member who has not prepared any material to present to the group. The other group members do not comment either. They are happy and excited to get on and share their ideas with their peers. The one group member who has not prepared a presentation sits quietly to begin with, then begins to join in. Towards the end of the session he shares his own ideas about how he plans to develop time management skills. The topic has now become the sole focus for the group. Kelly intervenes very little in the session although she does summarize and clarify points to enhance and develop understanding. At the end of the session, one group member refers to the fact that there is only one session remaining. Without Kelly's prompting, the group members discuss how they want to use the last session. Kelly suggests that perhaps some kind of 'celebration' to mark the ending of the group might be a good thing to do. After the session has ended, Kelly reflects on how effectively the group 'performed'. She compares the way the group worked with how they were in earlier sessions and she can identify a clear progression through the forming, storming, norming and performing stages.

The fifth and final stage of the group process is referred to as the adjourning (or sometimes the mourning) phase. Any environment where young people have shared experiences and feelings with their peers, sometimes taking risks in order to do so, is likely to have been a safe and trusting place. For some young people, a sense of safety and trust may be an unfamiliar feeling and, as a result, a powerful one. It is therefore important that this phase is acknowledged and that group members are encouraged to express their feelings about their experiences in the group, the learning they have gained from it and how they feel about the group coming to an end. The experience of 'ending' will inevitably raise issues for some young people, reminding them of previous endings in their lives, some of which may have been painful or traumatic. The role of the facilitator at this stage is to encourage group members to summarize and acknowledge what they have learned, both about the topic and about themselves, as a result of being in the group. The facilitator will also provide participants with the opportunity to explore their feelings about leaving the group by planning an 'ending' activity to the session. Kelly has now reached the final session with her group of six 15-year-olds. Let us see how effectively the 'adjourning' stage is managed.

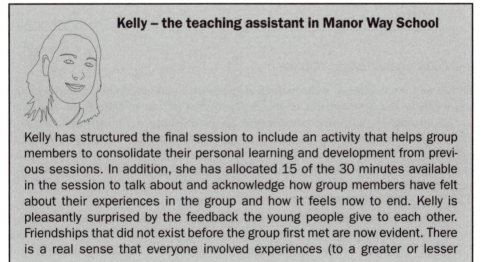

Kelly – the teaching assistant in Manor Way School

Kelly has structured the final session to include an activity that helps group members to consolidate their personal learning and development from previous sessions. In addition, she has allocated 15 of the 30 minutes available in the session to talk about and acknowledge how group members have felt about their experiences in the group and how it feels now to end. Kelly is pleasantly surprised by the feedback the young people give to each other. Friendships that did not exist before the group first met are now evident. There is a real sense that everyone involved experiences (to a greater or lesser extent) a sense of 'belonging' to the group and sadness that the meetings have now come to an end. Kelly closes the session (and the group) with an activity where she and each group member write something positive about every other person in the group. As a result, each young person leaves the group with six positive comments about themselves from their peers and their facilitator. As the young people leave, several speak to Kelly to thank her. Kelly is surprised to find herself feeling sad that the group has come to an end, but pleased that the sessions she had planned and facilitated have been successful, both in terms of meeting the topic objectives and the group process.

Knowledge and understanding of this chronological approach to group dynamics is helpful to youth support workers. It provides them with a theory on which to reflect while they are working with groups (particularly when they engage with the same group over a period of time). Instead of being anxious about, and ready to blame their own performance as facilitators, the practitioners will be aware that it is a recognized aspect of the group's development to progress through the 'storming' stage. Group members will 'test out' the skills of the facilitator in maintaining a safe and positive learning environment. Evolution of the group as an entity is a natural part of the process. An awareness of this helps the youth support worker to structure activities in order to support rather than challenge the group's development.

Activity

Reflect on two personal learning and development groups that you have been involved in. Using Tuckman's theory, establish which stage each group has reached in its development. What is happening in each group that characterizes the stage of its development? What might you do as facilitator to move both groups forward to the next stage?

Individual characteristic approach

So far, we have examined a chronological approach to understanding group dynamics, whereby the development of the group over a period of time from 'forming' to 'adjourning' is the prime determinant for establishing the group dynamic and analysing how the group and its members operate. An alternative approach to examining group dynamics, which takes account not just of the group process but of the characteristics of individual group members within it, is summarized by Vernelle who proposes that:

> A group is more than just the sum of its parts. That is, what happens in a group is not just the product of the individuals who are the members nor simply the result of the way it is set up. The impact of a group on individual members and

the influence of individuals on a group, goes round in circles, so that it is difficult to sort out who is influencing what at any given moment.

(Vernelle, 1994: 28)

Vernelle goes on to propose that most individuals in a group will take on a set of characteristics or 'role' that will influence their behaviour and responses. These roles are likely to be determined by features that include:

- physiological factors (age, gender, ethnicity);
- social factors (class, culture);
- previous experiences in groups;
- confidence and self-esteem;
- status with peers;
- additional learning needs.

For example, a small group of eight young people, which is made up of one young man and seven young women, is likely to possess a quite different dynamic to a group that consists of seven young men and one young woman. In each case the youth support worker will be instantly aware of how the gender balance is likely to have an impact on the group dynamic as the contributing characteristic (i.e. gender mix of the group) is highly visible. However, it is more difficult to recognize characteristics such as lack of confidence and self-esteem among group members. Indeed, often lack of confidence can present itself in a disguised form, with a group member 'acting up' or 'showing off' when, in fact, they lack the confidence to integrate in a group setting. The following example highlights the need for the youth support worker to be alert to a range of underlying factors that may influence the group dynamic.

Ade – a youth worker in Manor Way Youth Club

Ade has set up a small group for young people who have expressed an interest in learning about conflict resolution and self-defence skills. The group is made up of four young men and three young women. Ade has come into contact with each of the group members before, as they attend the youth club regularly. Most of the young people know each other, but not well. At the first session, Ade suggests that each group member shares their expectations for the group. What do they want to get out of these sessions? Everyone responds, but Ade notices that when one of the young women, Janine, speaks, two of the young men nudge each other and laugh. Janine ignores them and Ade does too to begin with, although he is aware that he must address behaviour that is excluding. Ade becomes increasingly aware that Janine, a normally chatty and open young woman, is withdrawn and quiet in the group. Later in the session, when Ade asks the young women to work together as a sub-group on an activity, one of the young men says, 'Janine should be with us, not with the girls'. Janine responds by punching the young man, who doubles up in pain. The other group members laugh and one of the young women says, 'I don't know why you're here Janine. You should be good at all this "boy" stuff'. Janine runs out of the session. Ade invites the group to explain their behaviour. It transpires that Janine is in a sexual relationship with another young woman and this has had an impact on the way that the other group members are responding to her. The dynamic of the group has been affected by the sexuality of one of its members. In fact, the member concerned has, for now, left the group altogether. Ade invites the group members to discuss their feelings about Janine's sexuality. He challenges their prejudices and a heated debate about sexuality ensues. Ade makes it clear to the group that their behaviour towards Janine is unacceptable. He also sees Janine separately after the session and invites her to return to the group.

This example demonstrates the significance of a range of individual factors (seen or unseen) that are likely to have an impact on the dynamic of the group. The incident in the example would not have taken place if Janine's sexuality had been unknown by the other group members. It is also likely that in a different group this would not have been an issue at all. However, in this case the individual factor of a group member's sexuality had a significant impact on the dynamic of the group and on the experience of one of its members.

Added to the complexity of attending to the individual factors and characteristics that may influence the group dynamic, the youth support worker should also be aware of the power of transference in the group (Freud, 1921), which may affect the way in which the group operates. In brief, the concept of transference relates to the ways in which we react and respond to each other, particularly in new or strange settings, by unconsciously looking for characteristics in others that are familiar to us or make us feel safe. These characteristics will be drawn from our own experiences of significant individuals (family figures or friends) in our lives. For example, if we feel safe in a group setting by 'taking the limelight' (because significant people in our lives have encouraged us to do so), then when we are in a new or strange setting, we may look for those in the group to whom we are unconsciously drawn to act as our 'audience'. We will relate to them as though they *are* our audience, thus encouraging a counter-transference response. This will involve the individuals concerned in (unwittingly, at times) playing their part in being our audience.

The example below illustrates transference and counter-transference in action in a PLD session with Pat, who works in a Pupil Referral Unit.

> ### Pat – the Pupil Referral Unit worker attached to Manor Way School
>
> Pat is working with a small group of young people in the unit, focusing on their anger management. There are five young people in the group, three young men and two young women, ranging from 14 to 16 years of age. Pat has met the group on a number of occasions and he has noticed that one participant, Wayne, tends to dominate group discussions. Initially, other group members tried to speak up in the sessions. Over time, however, Pat has become aware that when he asks a question of the group, the young people look straight to Wayne, who inevitably responds. Because Wayne unconsciously sought safety initially in a familiar role as 'spokesperson' at the centre of events (transference), Pat and the group members increasingly find themselves playing the role of audience, waiting for Wayne to speak (counter-transference). Pat is aware of this dynamic forming and he is also aware that all the group members are complicit (albeit unconsciously) in what is happening.

This example illustrates the need for youth support workers to use their active listening skills (see Chapter 7) to pick up verbal and behavioural clues, which offer insight into the roles that young people are consciously or unconsciously 'acting out' in the group.

Redl (1972) suggests some interesting titles for particular individual roles that may be evident in a group. Among others, he identifies:

- tyrant – dominating and bullying presence;
- fixer – trying to make everything in the group 'right';
- bad influence – disrupting and subverting others.

Vernelle (1994) adds to the list with:

- scapegoat – blaming or bullying an individual in the group;
- monopolizer – demanding attention of the group and the facilitator;
- trivializer – refusing to credit the session or the group as having any significance;
- silent critic – demonstrating disapproval through non-engagement.

She goes on to point out that not all the roles are negative or destructive in a group. For example, she recognizes the:

- good listener;

- calming influence;
- inspirer.

It is the role of the facilitator to recognize not only the behaviour (and therefore the role/label the behaviour translates into), but also to be mindful of the underlying factors that are influencing the behaviour. These factors, as already discussed, could relate to physiological, psychological or social traits (such as age, class, ethnicity or gender) or they could be present as a result of a process of transference and counter-transference. In either case, it is the responsibility of the youth support worker to be aware of, and to understand the underlying influences on the group dynamic. They also need to take action where necessary to ensure that the group is able to function effectively. Most important is the need to ensure that no individual suffers damage or harm as a result of the group dynamic.

Activity

Reflect on the same two groups that you used in the previous activity. This time use the individual characteristic approach to identify the influences on the group dynamic. Using Vernelle's terminology, try to identify group roles (scapegoat, inspirer, others)? Using your understanding of transference and counter-transference, how much might this concept be impacting on the group?

Summary

This chapter establishes what is meant by group dynamics, and enhances the youth support worker's understanding of the factors influencing the dynamic within groups. Two key theoretical approaches to group dynamics are introduced. First, the chronological approach is explained that emphasizes the stages of development through which each group progresses, and considers how the particular stage of development may influence the dynamic. Second, the individual characteristic approach is discussed which recognizes that any group is made up of a number of individuals who bring their unique traits, personalities and experiences. The 'mix' of individuals is what constitutes the group, and the dynamic of the group will depend largely on how the individuals respond to each other and work together.

Knowledge of group dynamics helps those who work with groups to analyse the reasons behind why individuals behave in particular ways in certain groups. In addition, it assists youth support workers to gain insight into groups that do not appear to 'gel' or seem to function in a state of conflict. Youth support workers should apply their understanding sensitively; after all they are not 'experts' in group dynamics, nor should they be. The facilitator should develop skills of active listening in order to attend not just to individuals, but also to the group itself. The role of the youth support worker is to acknowledge and celebrate 'difference' within the group, while at the same time cultivating a sense of group identity and ownership.

9

Managing challenging behaviour and attitudes

Learning Objectives

· Describe the concept of diversity

· Identify a range of challenging behaviours

· Establish strategies for working with challenging individuals, groups and situations

Introduction

This book has been structured in such a way that chapters can be accessed and read on a 'stand-alone' basis. In all probability, many readers are likely to have turned swiftly to this chapter as the subject of 'managing behaviour' is close to the heart of those who are involved in group work with young people. The rationale for placing this chapter towards the end of the book is simple. If youth support workers follow the suggestions made in earlier chapters concerning the planning, preparation and structuring of their group sessions, then the need for specific guidance on managing challenging behaviour is likely to be reduced significantly. If, as a result of the planning process, the needs of the group members have been assessed accurately; if the focus of the PLD group session is seen by participants to be of relevance; if the content of the session is engaging and stimulating; if the approach and skills used by the facilitator are student-centred and if attention is paid to the group dynamic, then problems with young people displaying challenging behaviour are pre-empted. So, the contents of this chapter should be viewed in context alongside the previous chapters in the book. When attention is paid to the preparation and planning of the session and the application of appropriate facilitation skills, then challenging behaviour is less likely to arise. Dunn supports this view:

> Many of the teachers I have known over the years who have had the most prob-
> lems engaging with youngsters have been those whose planning and preparation

has been the poorest. So being prepared, well planned and organized has as much to do with behaviour management as anything else.

(Dunn, 2005: 14)

Having said that, of course, it would be unrealistic to suggest that challenging situations will never arise. Even when thorough planning and preparation have taken place and excellent facilitation skills are in evidence, there will be times when even the most experienced youth support workers find themselves delivering sessions where challenges are presented that require action.

It is important, before going further, to stress that the role and responsibilities of youth support workers in relation to the context in which they work must be clearly understood. For example, teaching assistants, personal advisers, learning mentors and other youth support workers who are based in schools or educational establishments must familiarize themselves with the systems and policies in place for behaviour management, anti-bullying and discipline in their institution. They should also develop professional working relationships with subject teachers, form tutors and heads of year to ensure that they are supporting the work of the academic staff and the ethos of the institution.

So, youth support workers based in educational institutions should have a clear understanding of the policies and procedures with regard to behaviour management, sanctions and discipline. Although they may be working with small groups of young people away from the classroom, youth support workers should be aware of who, in the institution, has ultimate responsibility for the young people with whom they are working at any given time (this is likely to be a qualified teacher). Following occasions where behaviour in a group has been challenging, the youth support worker should report back to the teacher (or the person with ultimate responsibility for the students at that time), discuss the incident or behaviour, clarify the measures taken and seek advice on any further action required. A consistent and unified approach to group management is therefore taken, and the systems, policies and procedures within the institution are adhered to. Dunn emphasizes this point:

Do take time to learn the school systems for dealing with poor behaviour. Every school is different and it is vital that you familiarize yourself with all of these systems before your first encounter with any youngster. Not knowing these systems, and even worse not being able to apply them, puts you in a vulnerable and disadvantageous position.

(Dunn, 2005: 22)

This chapter strives to address the fears and fantasies of those youth support workers who are new to group work and have had very little or no training in behaviour management. At the same time, it aims to provide additional insight to those who are more experienced in delivering PLD group sessions. The chapter assesses a range of 'challenging' behaviours, establishing how the behaviours are recognized, and considering how they are managed effectively.

First, though, the chapter examines the concept of diversity. It should be stated clearly that the link between diversity and challenging behaviour is about understanding and managing 'difference' in the group. This is not to imply that a diverse group will be a challenging one, but rather that it is important to be aware of how diversity may contribute to group members' views about themselves and how they relate to each other. In particular, the chapter considers ways in which diversity within the group may impact on individual or group behaviour, and it establishes the role of the youth support worker in engaging actively with the diversity that exists in the group.

So, before we examine the different challenging behaviours that those who deliver PLD group sessions might face (drawing on case study examples to illustrate challenging behaviour and to demonstrate techniques for dealing with it), let us consider what is meant by diversity and establish how it may influence behaviour in groups.

What is diversity?

The concept of diversity is explored extensively in the literature (Brown, 1995; Blatchford, 1998; Sue and Sue, 1999; Kurland, 2002; Ali, 2003; Malekoff, 2004; Kehily, 2007) where meanings are sought for this complex theoretical concept. In simple terms (and it should be noted that the concept of diversity is neither simple, nor straightforward), diversity is all about the 'mix' of individuals in the group in relation to their race, ethnicity, culture, social class, gender, religion, dis/ability, sexuality, and so on. If we agree the definition of a group as an entity made up of a number of individuals, then within the group there will be aspects of identity that are shared among the group members (e.g. if a group consists of eight young men, then the group members have their *gender* in common). There may also be factors that are not common to the majority of the group, but are shared by a small number of young people within it (e.g. within the group of eight, three of the young men are black and share the same *ethnic* background). Furthermore, there may be a significant minority of the group who possess a distinctive feature or belief that is not shared by the vast majority of the group members (e.g. among the eight young men, one of the young people is a Muslim with a distinct *religious* identity, and another has a learning *disability*).

This difference or 'diversity' within the group is likely to provide a rich source of learning about ideas, views, values, beliefs, prejudices and tolerance among its members. Malekoff describes the way in which the group experience can offer its members the chance to embrace and understand fully what diversity means and how it impacts on their lives:

> A good group experience can provide adolescents with a unique opportunity to explore the typically taboo areas of race and ethnicity, exposing deeply ingrained or loosely formed beliefs and attitudes. The mature group, through the development of its own history and culture, becomes a special frame of reference for its members, influencing their perceptions and behaviour in the world outside of the group.
>
> (Malekoff, 2004: 207)

Malekoff suggests that the group itself can provide a dynamic forum for addressing issues of diversity and difference in a way that keeps group members safe. By being aware of and working to reduce stereotyping, an enhanced understanding and acceptance should develop. This is achieved by fostering a supportive environment in which every member has a voice, where each individual is entitled to a view and respect between peers develops. At times, however, it is their response to difference that causes conflict between young people. Social stereotypes and familial or class influences have an impact on how young people view each other and themselves in relation to their peers (Bruegel, 2005; Kehily, 2007). They may find certain elements of others' 'difference' difficult to understand or accept. They may feel fearful of, or threatened by, a feature, belief or behaviour that is at odds with their own (Coleman and Hendry, 1999). This prompts the question how might negative responses to diversity in a PLD session manifest themselves? The following suggestions exemplify ways in which young people may respond negatively to difference in a group setting:

- using discriminatory language;
- calling names and verbal bullying;
- engaging in excluding behaviour;
- displaying threatening behaviour (physical threats or violence).

When the responses to difference among group members are unacceptable (as outlined in the examples above), direct action by the youth support worker is required (we examine this later). But, to reduce the risk of these behaviours emerging, Malekoff (2004) suggests seven principles for addressing diversity in groups:

1 Refer to issues of diversity as a positive and normal aspect of group development and identity.

2 Raise awareness of current or recent local, national or global events in which issues of diversity have played a part.

3 Challenge prejudice and stereotyping immediately.

4 Be aware of our own identity and how this may impact on the group. Engender a respectful climate in the group.

5 Help to broaden awareness of the values and beliefs of others.

6 Enable understanding that being part of a particular ethnic group (for example) does not mean that these group members are the 'same' as each other.

7 Highlight similarities and commonalities across different groups.

These principles are both sound and helpful, and if adhered to, are likely to foster a positive approach to diversity. Thus, it is the role of the youth support worker to address the differences among group members from an enabling standpoint, modelling an open and supportive approach to working with diversity within the group. Where the relationship between the youth support worker and the group is grounded in student-centred principles based on honesty, respect and trust, the young people will be encouraged to foster a curious and non-judgemental approach to exploring what diversity means for them. This will enable them to accept that difference within a group enriches rather than threatens their experience.

Of course, as stated earlier, the presence of a diverse mix of young people in PLD sessions does not predetermine challenging behaviour. Quite the reverse, in fact. In many cases, particularly where young people have experienced diversity throughout their education and lives, difference is often accepted, understood and celebrated (or, at the very least, tolerated). A visit to a group of young people from an ethnically diverse area, where for many English is not their first language, will soon demonstrate how quickly and flexibly young people are able to work with and support difference in a positive way. It is the 'norm' and is therefore not unfamiliar or threatening (Bruegel, 2005).

However, there will be occasions when the unacceptable behaviours identified earlier may occur. This can happen even though the youth support worker adheres to the principles set out above, as a response to a threat or fear connected with difference. Challenging behaviour resulting from a range of causes, and the ways in which the practitioner can respond to challenging behaviour, will now be explored.

What is challenging behaviour and why does it happen?

When the subject of 'challenging' behaviour is raised, responses to it vary enormously. These responses depend on our own definitions of what constitutes behaviour that is challenging. For example, some youth support workers may tolerate, or even be unaware of, high noise levels in PLD sessions. Others will find any noise above a gentle murmur to be distracting and unhelpful. Rogers illustrates the point:

> It is not easy to rate a disruption as 'low', 'medium' or 'high level'. To one teacher pen-tapping may be no problem; something which can be ignored. But if it is persistent, pen-tapping, on a hot day, in the middle of an important explanation by the teacher, can be quite a different matter.
>
> (Rogers, 1998: 52)

Whether or not behaviour is deemed to be challenging depends on a number of factors. These include the responses of the other group members to the behaviour, the level of experience of the facilitator, the confidence of the facilitator, the skills of the facilitator, the context in which the group work is taking place and the physical circumstances (e.g. location of the session, temperature in the room or use/breakdown of technology). However, there is undoubtedly some behaviour that to a greater or lesser extent would challenge any facilitator, however experienced, skilled or confident. It is this behaviour that we concentrate on now. The list below suggests some of the most common forms of challenging behaviour that youth support workers are likely to encounter at some point in their work:

- shouting out;
- refusing to cooperate/be involved;
- swearing or using abusive language;
- 'clowning around' (throwing things, making noises, distracting others);
- giggling or chatting consistently through the session;
- bullying – verbal;

- bullying – physical/aggressive behaviour;
- making comments based on stereotypes (sexist/racist remarks)
- appearing tired, unhappy or distracted;
- withdrawing, looking frightened or apprehensive and not wanting to be involved.

Rogers describes many of these behaviours as being attention or power seeking:

> One of the central needs a person has is to be noticed: to be attended to, to have contact with others. Most students fulfil this need in socially acceptable ways: they put their hands up, they ask for equipment instead of snatching, they wait their turn, they gain positive attention through the production of acceptable work, they participate co-operatively: they 'belong'.
>
> (Rogers, 1998: 28)

He goes on to explain that some young people may resort to less positive strategies to 'belong' or be noticed in a group. These strategies may be habitual and have been developed as a result of experiences in childhood. They may be centred on a desire to be noticed and to crave some form of attention (regardless of whether this is positive or negative). They may be borne out of a need to seek power; as it may be that when the young person is in a position of power, they feel as though they belong and have established their safe and familiar place in the group.

There are, of course, less overt types of challenging behaviour and different reasons why young people exhibit it. For example, some young people may work very hard *not* to be noticed in a group. A quiet and seemingly withdrawn demeanour may simply indicate a reflective learning style (see Chapter 2), but it could also suggest a range of other personal, learning or mental health issues that the young person is experiencing. Young people who are facing these types of difficulty may simply want to go unnoticed and not draw attention to their presence within the group.

Outside influences can also play their part in generating challenging behaviour. For example, drugs or alcohol consumed at lunch-time are likely to have an adverse effect on behaviour during a PLD session in the afternoon. Similarly, a young person, who has stayed awake all night playing computer games, is unlikely to engage in the session and may exhibit challenging behaviour (like yawning or falling asleep).

Whatever the challenging behaviour or its cause, one thing is clear; the youth support worker has a responsibility to take action to ensure that a safe and supportive environment is established and maintained. This is crucial in order that personal learning and development for all group members takes place.

Strategies for managing challenging behaviour

When faced with challenging behaviour, there may be a temptation for the youth support worker to respond immediately (or not respond at all) without first 'thinking through' the situation. This is risky and could result in the following consequences:

- taking inappropriate action;
- 'punishing' the wrong person;

- becoming embroiled in a no-win situation;
- colluding with the behaviour;
- losing credibility;
- losing their temper;
- not providing support when it is needed;
- damaging the relationship between the group and themselves.

Undertaking (albeit quickly) an assessment of what is happening in the room is critical. When faced with what appears to be challenging or disruptive behaviour, the youth support worker should not take action without first asking themselves five questions:

1   What is the behaviour (what does it look like, sound like, feel like)?
2   What are the reasons behind the behaviour (attention seeking, belonging, learning needs, mental health issues and so on)?
3   What am I doing/not doing that may be contributing to the behaviour (am I being clear, am I listening, am I making myself understood, am I establishing appropriate boundaries)?
4   Who is the behaviour affecting (the individual concerned, others in the group, me)?
5   Are the session objectives 'at risk' if the behaviour continues?

Reflecting on these questions will enable the facilitator to analyse the situation and respond in a way that is measured, objective and appropriate. Attending to the questions will provide some 'space' and thinking time, ensuring that the risk of an inappropriate or harmful response is minimized. Most importantly, it will help to inform a judgement based on an understanding of what is contributing to the behaviour and the impact of the behaviour on other group members and the session objectives.

Question

If the answers to the five questions outlined above are as follows, what action should the facilitator take?

---

1   What is the behaviour? A young person is constantly getting up and walking around the room.
2   What is behind the behaviour? Attention seeking and concentration difficulties.
3   What am I doing/not doing that may be contributing to the behaviour? Becoming increasingly distracted and irritated by the behaviour, but not addressing it directly.
4   Who is the behaviour affecting? Me. Other group members are familiar with the behaviour from this particular individual and are not bothered or distracted by it.

5   Are the session objectives 'at risk'? No. The rest of the group are engaging with the activities while the young person concerned is opting in and out.

If sufficient attention is *not* paid to the questions above, one response to this scenario might be to react by approaching the 'wanderer', and asking them to sit down and join the group. Then, if the behaviour continues, the facilitator might make the decision to ignore it, as constantly attending to it will detract from the session for the rest of the group. An alternative approach (again, ignoring the questions above) might be to challenge the individuals every time they get up and walk around the room, demanding that they sit down and join in with their peers. This is likely to result in increased frustration and distraction for the facilitator who stops paying adequate attention to the rest of the group.

Both responses are risky. In the former, the message given to the group members is that unacceptable behaviour will be noticed. However, it also suggests that the boundaries in the group can be broken without being challenged consistently (the risk here being that other group members might also take the opportunity to do as they please in the session). If the latter approach is adopted, much of the facilitator's time is likely to be taken up with the disruptive group member; the worst-case scenario being that a 'stand-off' between the facilitator and the disruptive member may occur. There is, of course, a third way to respond to this behaviour, which pays close attention to the answers to the five questions outlined above. Clearly, the behaviour does not appear to be having a detrimental impact on either the group members or the session objectives. However, it is an attention-seeking and potentially disruptive behaviour that should be attended to. If the youth support worker responds by using the activities planned for the session flexibly, thus engaging and involving the disruptive group member at all times, then the need for the young person to get up and move around is ameliorated. Activities could be shortened in length, small groups might be regularly changed or more 'pair work' could be instigated. In addition, if a contract has been agreed at the outset, this could be revisited in the light of the behaviour and new ground rules agreed with the group as a whole.

As well as taking time to analyse and reflect on the behaviour before responding, there are some additional guidelines or 'dos and don'ts' to group management that should underpin all PLD group work. These are:

- Remember that young people are human beings with rights and responsibilities. They are not lesser mortals and we do not have any rights to treat them as such.

- Be clear about your role and your boundaries and communicate with the group with these in mind. You are not a teacher, but neither are you their best friend.

- Agree a contract (ground rules) at the outset (see Chapter 6). The ground rules concerning behaviour and other group norms are suggested, agreed by all group members and written up. The contract provides a helpful resource to return to during the session if the rules are breached.

- Learn and use the names of group members. We all respond more positively to being called by name rather than 'oi you!'

- Speak to young people's faces, not their backs. In many cases an appropriate facial expression (e.g. a raised eyebrow) will be enough of a message to halt a group member who is being disruptive. Non-verbal signals are powerful, but they will not work if they are not visible to the intended recipient.

- Use praise rather than criticism where possible. For example, when young people are not concentrating on their work and trying to distract other group members, praise the group members who are focusing; 'that's great. I'm hearing some really fantastic ideas from this group' rather than 'come on Mark. How come it's always you who is disrupting everybody else?' Most of us respond better to praise than criticism. If we see and hear others getting praise, we are likely to want some.

- Challenge the behaviour, not the person. For example, 'we agreed at the start of the session that there would be no shouting/moving around/throwing things/fighting. Let's make sure that it stops now and doesn't happen again' rather than 'Joe, you're such a pain. I knew you would be at the centre of this'.

- Look for solutions to disruptive behaviour with young people rather than focus on the reasons for it. For example, 'I need the giggling to cease now, thanks' rather than 'why do you keep giggling and disrupting the class?'

- Avoid the use of sarcasm or belittling language. Making a group member feel small does not fit with the core conditions of a student-centred response.

- Use inclusive language when challenging behaviour. For example, 'we need to make sure that we keep on track here. We're not going to do that if there is constant shouting in the room'.

- Be clear and consistent in your responses to challenging behaviour. If you draw attention to one person who is chatting in the group, you must ensure that you do not ignore others who are doing the same. Most young people have a keen sense of fair play and will feel, very quickly, as though they are being 'picked on' if messages are not given consistently.

- Use humour carefully; it is a useful tool for diffusing or lightening potentially 'heavy' situations, but the line between humour and sarcasm is a fine one and sarcasm, by its nature, can be belittling.

- Do not make empty threats that you have no intention of carrying out. For example, when you say, 'if you do that one more time you will be leaving this room', you must stick to it!

- Use a system of incremental disciplinary measures so that you have 'somewhere to go'. For example, 'I'm asking you now for the first time. If we need to have this conversation again, I will ask you to leave the group. What can we do to make sure that is not going to happen?'

- Do not make assumptions about individual behaviour. A young person who appears to be tired and unfocused may have a chaotic and difficult home life to deal with rather than simply be suffering from too many late nights.

- Respond sensitively to young people who appear to be shy and withdrawn in the session. Avoid singling them out, but assist them to feel comfortable by including them in activities and speaking to them separately if appropriate.

Let us return to some of the youth support workers we have met throughout the book, and observe how they are managing challenging behaviour in their PLD group sessions.

Kelly – the teaching assistant in Manor Way School

Kelly is working with a number of groups in the school at the request of teachers or heads of year. In one group of six young people (three young women and three young men aged 13) she has experienced challenging behaviour. The group have met together for a number of sessions. The students have exhibited disruptive behaviour in their maths lessons. The maths teacher has asked Kelly to work with the group to focus on behaviour management skills. Kelly has planned a programme of short PLD sessions about developing better communication skills.

The third session has started and one of the students, Chris, is using his ruler as a catapult, firing balls of wet paper at other group members.

Josie: Ouch! That really hurt. Kelly. Did you see what Chris just did?
Chris: Shut up you fat cow!
(rest of the group laugh)

Question
How would you respond to Chris's behaviour?

(Kelly turns to address Chris directly)
Kelly: OK. Two things here Chris. First, you have a choice. Either the ruler goes back in your bag now or you can give it to me to look after until we've finished. Second, the way you spoke to Josie was unacceptable.
(Kelly turns to the group)
Kelly: What did we agree when we started these sessions about how we wanted each other to behave?
(silence)
Kelly: Do you remember, we agreed a set of rules. What did they say?
Josie: Not to be disrespectful to each other.
Chris: I wasn't being disrespectful you fat cow, I was telling the truth!
(everyone laughs)
Kelly: What you have said to Kelly twice now *is* disrespectful, Chris. It's unacceptable and if I hear that kind of personal remark again I will ask you to leave this group.
(Kelly turns to the group)

> **Kelly**: The point of these sessions is to think about the ways in which we communicate with each other. What we've just heard is unkind and hurtful. If we use that kind of language to each other, how does it make us feel?

Kelly does well to challenge Chris's behaviour immediately. She does not simply respond to the physical behaviour but attends to the verbal bullying too. Kelly wants to deal with the incident swiftly so that there is minimum disruption to her session. She also takes the opportunity to make a point about unacceptable behaviour to all group members. By making the link between Chris's behaviour and the topic of the PLD session (communication skills), Kelly is reinforcing learning about what is acceptable and not acceptable when communicating. Following the session, Kelly has a short talk with Chris and explains that she will be reporting the incident to his form tutor and his maths tutor. This conforms to the school disciplinary policy.

In another incident, Pat, working in the Pupil Referral Unit, is delivering a PLD session on assertiveness to eight young people whose ages range from 13 to 16.

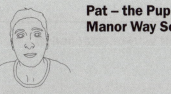

Pat – the Pupil Referral Unit worker attached to Manor Way School

Pat asks the young people to work together in two small groups. Natalie refuses to work in a group with Jack.

Natalie: No way am I working with him. No way. Not after last time. I'll leave this session if you make me work in his group.

Jack: Yeah, and you think I want to work with you? Get a life!

Natalie: Why can't I work with Charelle and that lot? Jack's just going to stir up trouble like he did last time.

Jack: Oh shut your face! What's your problem anyway you slag?

Charelle: Leave her alone. You think you're so hard don't you?

Jack: Keep your nose out of it. What's it got to do with you anyway you interfering cow?

Question
What would you do if you were Pat?

Pat: OK. That's enough. Natalie, move yourself into Jack's group now. This has taken up far too much time already.

Natalie: No.

Pat: Natalie. Do what I've said and move now.

Charelle: You can't make her move if she doesn't want to.

Jack: I told you to keep your nose out of it.

(Charelle gets out of her chair and walks across to stand over Jack)

> **Charelle**: (threateningly) What's it got to do with you, hard man?
> (Jack pushes Charelle, and she pushes him back. The rest of the group move out of their seats and gather round, chanting 'fight, fight, fight')
> **Pat**: Right that's it. Jack, Charelle, come outside with me now. The rest of you sit down, the show's over, get on with your work.

Although situations like this are rare, stand-offs with group members can occur, and as we see in this example, they can escalate swiftly into a potentially dangerous scenario. Pat resolved the situation eventually by removing the disruptive young people and dealing with them separately, away from the group. There is nothing wrong with this (in fact, it is helpful to diffuse escalating situations by removing the cause of the disruption), but while Pat is outside talking to Jack and Charelle, the rest of the group are left to their own devises and it is unlikely that any learning about assertiveness is taking place. In situations such as this, it is crucial that the youth support worker intervenes early. In this case the interaction between Natalie, Jack and Charelle goes unchallenged for some time. Let us see how it might have been managed differently.

Pat – the Pupil Referral Unit worker attached to Manor Way School

Pat asks the young people to work together in two small groups. Natalie refuses to work in a group with Jack.

Natalie: No way am I working with him. No way. Not after last time. I'll leave this session if you make me work in his group.

Jack: Yeah, and you think I want to work with you? Get a life!

Pat: Whoa! Let's stop right there and remind ourselves about how we agreed to behave with each other. Respect, if I remember rightly! Remember too, that the topic of these sessions is 'assertiveness'. Last time we met we talked about the problems with communicating aggressively rather than assertively. How could Natalie have expressed herself in an assertive way so that Jack wouldn't have been tempted to respond rudely and aggressively as he did then?

(silence)

Pat: Any ideas? Lauren?

Lauren: Erm . . . Natalie could've said, 'Jack and me don't get on and I'd rather work with Charelle and that lot'.

(A discussion ensues about communicating assertively rather than aggressively. The discussion ends with Natalie asking assertively not to work in Jack's group. Pat agrees with the request on this occasion and the session moves on.)

In the second example, Pat responds by:

- intervening early;
- referring back to the group contract;
- linking the incident to the topic under discussion in order to extract learning from it.

Although it could be argued that Pat 'gave way' by allowing Natalie not to work with Jack, he assessed the situation and decided that it would be more helpful to avoid a stand-off by challenging the behaviour, linking it to the topic and ending, as far as possible, with a win-win situation. Ignoring conflict does not make it go away. It is challenging for the youth support worker, but can energize the group if it is used to provide a positive learning experience.

In the third case study, we return to a session we visited earlier in the book with Ashraf, who is working with a class-sized group of young people aged 13. The session is focusing on the support available to students within and outside the school.

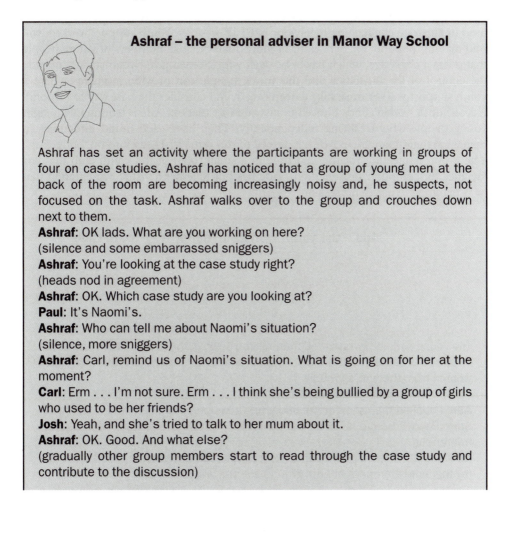

Ashraf – the personal adviser in Manor Way School

Ashraf has set an activity where the participants are working in groups of four on case studies. Ashraf has noticed that a group of young men at the back of the room are becoming increasingly noisy and, he suspects, not focused on the task. Ashraf walks over to the group and crouches down next to them.

Ashraf: OK lads. What are you working on here?
(silence and some embarrassed sniggers)
Ashraf: You're looking at the case study right?
(heads nod in agreement)
Ashraf: OK. Which case study are you looking at?
Paul: It's Naomi's.
Ashraf: Who can tell me about Naomi's situation?
(silence, more sniggers)
Ashraf: Carl, remind us of Naomi's situation. What is going on for her at the moment?
Carl: Erm . . . I'm not sure. Erm . . . I think she's being bullied by a group of girls who used to be her friends?
Josh: Yeah, and she's tried to talk to her mum about it.
Ashraf: OK. Good. And what else?
(gradually other group members start to read through the case study and contribute to the discussion)

> **Ashraf**: That's great lads. Right, what does the case study ask you to do now? Have a read through, and move on to the next discussion point. Keep the ideas coming!

Ashraf tackles the potentially disruptive behaviour by moving across the classroom to work directly with the small group. He physically crouches down to their level so that he does not tower above them. The power of the use of physicality and body language should not be underestimated. Of course, it is not appropriate to touch or threaten individuals physically. But being in close proximity to the young people concerned, thereby letting them know that you *are* aware of what is going on, is likely to have an impact on levels of disruption. Ashraf also addresses individuals by name. Although he has not worked with this group before, he has asked them to make name badges that they wear on their jackets. Ashraf is aware that this 'opens the door' for a 'Mickey Mouse' or 'Lara Croft' in the room, but generally he thinks that it is useful to be able to address group members directly by name.

In each of the examples outlined in this chapter, a different scenario has been used to illustrate challenging behaviour in PLD sessions. Youth support workers will find that it is not only the behaviour of individuals or small numbers of young people that poses a challenge, which has to be dealt with. Sometimes, circumstances outside the control of the facilitator and the young people can provide moments where a youth support worker must take a deep breath and consider the best way to respond. Ade, a youth worker, finds himself in just such a situation. Ade is working with eight young people who are living independently. They have each found difficulties in managing their finances, so Ade has agreed to run some PLD sessions on 'budgeting'. The group is meeting for the first time in a small room in the youth club that has facilities for computer presentations. Ade has put together a visual presentation that he is planning to use in his session.

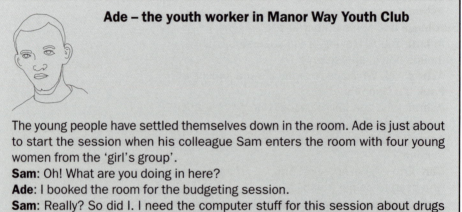

Ade – the youth worker in Manor Way Youth Club

The young people have settled themselves down in the room. Ade is just about to start the session when his colleague Sam enters the room with four young women from the 'girl's group'.
Sam: Oh! What are you doing in here?
Ade: I booked the room for the budgeting session.
Sam: Really? So did I. I need the computer stuff for this session about drugs awareness.
Ade: Yeah. Me too. I booked this room for the same reason.
(by this time members of both groups are starting to call out 'get on with it!')

Ade: OK. How long do you need the room for?

Sam: 20 minutes, tops. Then we can go elsewhere.

Ade: All right. I can cut my session down from an hour, to 40 minutes. This will give you the chance to come in at the end to do your 20 minutes.

Sam: Cheers mate!

(Sam and the girls leave the room and Ade switches on the computer and the projector. Unfortunately, the light on the projector does not come on despite Ade's lengthy attempts to make it do so. By now, half of the group members have wandered off for a game of football and the other half stay in the room and laugh at Ade's fruitless attempts to make the technology work)

Question

What could have been done to ensure that the challenging situation with the double-booked room did not arise, and that the situation with the technology was dealt with more effectively?

It is always important to double-check arrangements that have been made to ensure that the group is in the right place at the right time, the venue is appropriate and available, the length of the session has been made clear, the numbers of young people who arrive for the session correspond to the numbers for whom the session was planned, and so on. In addition, if technology is being used, it is important to check it first and to have a back-up plan in case of emergencies. For example, if the session includes showing a 30-minute DVD and the TV is not in the room or is broken, then it is important that the youth support worker has planned another activity that can be used instead. In the example above, Ade could have printed out his presentation on handouts and used these as a visual aid when the technology let him down.

Summary

Two areas have been examined in this chapter: the concept of diversity and what it means to work with 'difference' and the subject of behaviour management. Although it was stated at the outset that the need for managing challenging behaviour should be significantly reduced if planning and preparation have been carried out thoroughly, it is nevertheless true to say that the youth support worker who never encounters challenging behaviour in PLD sessions is a rare individual. The chapter has described 'typical' challenging behaviour (both passive and aggressive), and it has provided some insight into why young people might exhibit these behaviours and attitudes. It has gone on to establish some practical measures for addressing challenging behaviour and unforeseen situations in PLD sessions. Table 9.1 on pages 144–5 summarizes a range of challenging behaviours and suggests appropriate responses to them.

To conclude, it is important to emphasize that the literature referred to in this chapter has been written with teachers in mind. Indeed, there is very little written about managing group behaviour in educational settings that is not directed at teachers. Although it would be useful to access the literature that is available and read more about the subject, youth support workers should remind themselves that they are *not* teachers. Personal learning and development is grounded in a collaborative or facilitative, student-centred ethos. The need to build a relationship of trust with group members and understand young people is paramount. In most cases youth support workers are working with small groups, discussing subjects that are of direct personal relevance and interest to the participants. This should provide a conducive environment in which conflict and challenge is minimized.

Activity

Reflect on a recent group work where there was conflict or challenging behaviour and talk to an experienced colleague about your experience.

- What was the behaviour?
- How did you manage it?

Having reflected on the situation in the light of your developed understanding and your discussion with a colleague, what might you have done differently, and why?

Table 9.1 Responses to challenging behaviour

Challenging behaviour	Appropriate response
Shouting out	First, refer to the contract agreed at the start of the session, 'remember we said that we wouldn't shout out or speak over each other in this session'. If the behaviour continues, challenge the individual directly, 'Steven, remember what we agreed, no more shouting please'.
Refusing to cooperate, not wanting to be involved	Use the skill of immediacy (see Chapter 7) to open a dialogue to challenge the behaviour, 'it seems that you're finding it hard to join in with the group. How can we make it easier for you?' Use more interactive exercises – perhaps small group or pair work. Adding an element of 'competition' or a 'game' in the session can often motivate reluctant individuals
Swearing or using abusive, bullying and stereotyped language (e.g. sexist or racist remarks)	First, refer to the contract, 'remember we agreed not to swear in this session. Let's make sure that the swearing stops now'. If the language is abusive and bullying, or personal remarks are made to another member in the group, a strong challenge is required, 'Tom, what you just said to Carly is rude and disrespectful. This group won't tolerate any kind of personal or unkind comment. So, stop it now please'. If the behaviour continues or if the language is racist, sexist or damaging in other ways, then stronger sanctions may be needed. These must be informed by the disciplinary code in the institution and reported back as appropriate after the session has ended
'Clowning around', giggling or chatting through the session	Avoid the temptation to 'put down', or ridicule the behaviour. If the 'clowning' involves throwing things, making noises or distracting others, it is helpful to move physically closer to the perpetrator. It is more difficult for a young person to throw something across the room under the nose of the facilitator. The same applies to a group of 'chatterers' or 'gigglers'. Involving the group members in interesting and relevant activities that require focus and interaction will help. Beware 'separating' gigglers or chatterers. This can degenerate into a battle of wills between facilitator and group member; it can be time consuming and ultimately damaging to the success of the session

Threatening or aggressive behaviour	A direct challenge should be made at once. In the first instance, take the perpetrator(s) to one side and speak to them about what they have just said/done. If two people are involved (e.g. a fight is developing), then try to calm the situation down by speaking quietly and, if possible, arbitrating between those involved. If the individual(s) is not acting rationally and is beginning to lose control, it is important that facilitators attend to their own well-being and to the safety of the rest of the group members. This may mean excluding the aggressive group member(s), taking the other group members away from the potentially harmful situation or sending a reliable group member for help. Intervening between two group members who have lost control and are fighting is a potentially dangerous situation and should be avoided
Withdrawing. Looking frightened or apprehensive and not wanting to be involved. Appearing tired, unhappy or distracted	At an early point in the session, when students are involved in activities, speak to the young person concerned. Crouch down to their level to ensure that good eye contact and active listening can take place, without appearing threatening. Ask open questions to ascertain why the student is feeling uncomfortable in the session. It may be that, with encouragement, the young person is happy to become involved, perhaps in a small group or pair activity. There may, however, be more complex issues or problems that will need to be addressed outside the session. Support may need to be sought or referrals made to other professionals as appropriate
Specific learning difficulties or young people for whom English is not their first language	When working with students with learning or language needs, it is important to ascertain as much information as possible about the nature of the need before the session. Activities can then be planned which are appropriate and accessible to everyone in the group. It is important to give clear and concise verbal instructions (and support these with visual cues if appropriate). Often, other young people in the group will offer help and support to the group member who has additional needs

10

Evaluating personal learning and development

Learning Objectives

· Define the concept of evaluation

· Describe how evaluation applies to the session objectives, structure and outcomes

· Identify the relationship between evaluation and reflective practice

· Describe a range of evaluation methods

Introduction

It is fitting that this final chapter focuses on the process of evaluation. So far in this book, a logical step-by-step approach to planning, preparing and delivering PLD group sessions has been taken. This began by establishing the importance of assessing the needs of group members and identifying a topic, moving on to setting an aim and objectives for the session, planning activities, and so on. Although the PLD session is now drawing to a close, with group dynamics established and challenging behaviour managed effectively, the youth support worker cannot take the opportunity to sit back and relax. The benefits of evaluation should not be underestimated as it provides the following:

● An opportunity for young people to reflect on and clarify their learning.

● An opportunity for young people to identify further learning and support needs.

● A useful way for the youth support worker to analyse the effectiveness of the session and their own approach to facilitation.

● A starting point for considering how the session can be developed.

● An analysis, if appropriate, of how a particular session fits into an overall programme.

- An opportunity to build youth support workers' confidence in delivering PLD sessions.

This chapter begins by establishing the meaning of evaluation and examines its relationship to PLD sessions. It considers *why* evaluation is a valuable activity and *what* should be evaluated. It goes on to suggest *how* evaluation might take place. For example, if a thorough planning process has been undertaken using the FAAST model, there will be a set of session objectives (linked to the aim) that should have been achieved. To what extent these objectives have been met requires evaluation. Through the process of evaluation, it may become apparent that, for example, the objectives were inappropriate or unachievable and they should be reviewed and amended if a similar session is to be delivered again. In addition, the success of the group work is not determined simply by whether or not the participants have enjoyed it (although this is important). It is what the young people have achieved in terms of verifiable outcomes following the session that it is important to assess. Undertaking an evaluation activity should help to clarify these outcomes. Furthermore, the youth support worker has put in place a structure for the session and planned activities within it. The effectiveness of these are subject to evaluation too as adjustments to planning and delivery may be required. Finally, youth support workers have used a range of skills and techniques in order to facilitate learning during sessions and it is important that they have the opportunity to reflect on these in order to assess their effectiveness and identify areas of development that may be required.

First, the chapter establishes clearly what is meant by the term 'evaluation' and why it is important before moving on to examine the key areas outlined above and listed here where evaluation should take place:

- session objectives;
- outcomes;
- session structure and activities;
- facilitator's performance (skills and techniques).

The chapter goes on to introduce a range of methods that can be used in order to evaluate PLD sessions, including questionnaires and other evaluation activities.

What is evaluation and why is it important?

The process of evaluation is central to any planned activity. It is only by reflecting on and evaluating their PLD group sessions that youth support workers will have the opportunity to develop their practice, amend their group work to ensure greater learning potential for participants and build their own confidence. Clifford and Herrmann make the point that:

> The evaluation is another vital element of the process – without evaluation and

analysis there is no real learning, and no awareness of transformation. Evaluation consolidates what has been learnt.

(Clifford and Herrmann, 1999: 197)

Not only does evaluation consolidate what has been learned, as Clifford and Herrmann suggest, but it is also part of an ongoing process of learning, whereby key issues for further exploration will emerge and future PLD sessions or learning opportunities may be developed as a result.

The activity of evaluation involves *reflecting* on all aspects of the PLD group session, and it is therefore important for youth support workers to have an understanding of what reflection means and how it happens.

Reflective practice

The concept of reflective practice has been widely examined in the literature (Boud et al., 1985; Schon, 1990; Lowery, 2003; Bolton, 2005) and is likely to be familiar to most youth support workers. In brief, reflection requires a deep level of critical thinking about something that has taken place. This thinking then informs decisions and actions about future practice. Reflective thinking is more than simply asking the question 'what happened?' It requires analysis of 'what happened' by exploring 'how' and 'why' it happened. This analysis ensures that informed decisions are made and appropriate action is then taken. Engaging in reflective practice with respect to evaluating PLD group work can be undertaken by focusing on six key questions:

1   What were the events that took place? (What actually happened in the PLD group session?)

2   What worked well? (How effective was the structure, how engaging were the activities, and why?)

3   What could be left out or changed? (What did not go as planned, which activities could be changed and why?)

4   How did the facilitator feel and participate during the session? (Anxious? Confident? What did they do and why?)

5   How did the group engage? (Actively? Reluctantly? Fully? Partially? and why?)

6   How far were the session objectives met? (If they were not met or only partially met, what could have been done differently to ensure that they were fully met? Or were the objectives inappropriate or unrealistic to begin with?)

Thinking reflectively is a skill that some practitioners find relatively easy and others need to work harder to develop. Kolb's (1984) reflective learning cycle, introduced in Chapter 2, summarizes the process of learning through reflecting on experience. Honey and Mumford's (2000) learning styles (also explained in Chapter 2), identifies a 'reflector' learning preference that is dominant in some of us. Those who naturally adopt a reflective approach to their work are likely to engage in reflection and evaluation as a matter of course. Others, perhaps with more activist learning styles, may find it harder to set time aside to engage in formal critical reflection on their PLD session. Some, of course, might feel so relieved that the session is over that they simply want to 'move on' to the next thing and forget all about it!

Whatever the learning preference of the youth support worker happens to be, two points are clear:

1   Evaluation of PLD sessions should take place.
2   Evaluation cannot happen without reflection.

Of course, youth support workers will not only reflect on their PLD sessions once they have come to an end. They will also be using reflective skills throughout each group work to evaluate situations as they occur (reflecting 'in action') (Schon, 1990), to make judgements about activities that need to be simplified or extended, to enable all students to engage with their learning and to ensure that the session objectives are met. However, the focus of this chapter is on the evaluation that should take place at the end of the PLD session (reflecting 'on action') (Schon, 1990). So, what should be evaluated and what mechanisms and tools can be used to help evaluation to take place?

What should be evaluated?

As identified at the start of this chapter, there are four key aspects of PLD group sessions that require evaluating in order to analyse the effectiveness of the session and to inform subsequent development. The first of these are the session objectives that have been set prior to the group work taking place.

The session objectives

The importance of setting objectives for each PLD session was explored in detail in Chapter 4. To recap, the session objectives are a set of statements that describe what the participants have the opportunity to achieve in the session. The acronym PHOTO (Participants Have the Opportunity TO) is a helpful reminder when setting objectives. It suggests that the objectives include active, 'doing' words that are verifiable. For example:

- participants have the opportunity to *describe* how they feel;
- Participants have the opportunity to *write down* their options.

The youth support worker will then develop activities in order to ensure that participants *do* have the opportunity to meet the objectives. Evaluation of the session objectives should therefore be a comparatively straightforward activity. If we take the two objectives outlined above, it should be evident that if the youth support worker has included activities in the session that involve 'discussing feelings' and 'writing down options', then the objectives should be achieved. It is helpful though to take additional measures to examine how far the objectives have been met. Knowing that activities have been planned that directly address the objectives will go some way to ensuring that they are reached. But the *extent* to which the participants feel they have achieved the objectives and how relevant and useful the objectives were to them in the first place has not been established. There are a number of ways that the achievement of the objectives can be evaluated during the session:

- Share the objectives with the participants at the start of the session and return to them at the end. Use open questions to engage in a discussion about how far the objectives were met and how useful the session has been to them.
- Use a range of evaluation tools/methods (these are examined in more detail later in this chapter) that ask participants to comment, among other things, on the relevance and achievement with regard to the session objectives.
- Make links at appropriate points in the session when activities are being intro-duced, between the content of the activity and the objective to which it relates. Thus, participants will be clear about exactly what they are achieving in the session.

Implementing any of these suggestions will contribute towards a detailed and thor-ough evaluation of the session objectives. Moreover, it will provide the opportunity for participants to reflect on and specify the learning they have achieved within the group. It may be that further development is needed by the youth support worker in response to the comments made by the participants. Perhaps the session objectives were not as relevant or meaningful to the group as the facilitator had anticipated. Maybe there were too many objectives to achieve realistically during the session. It might become evident that the activities planned did not directly address the session object-ives at all, so they were never likely to be met. In each case, the youth support worker will have a clear sense of what they need to do next to ensure that the session is revised to meet the needs of future participants more fully. So, what else in addition to the specific preset session objectives requires evaluation? Where the *objectives* suggest what should be achieved *during* the session, the *outcomes* measure the impact of the learning *following* the session. The outcomes, like the objectives require evalu-ation, but, for obvious reasons, evaluation of the outcomes cannot take place in the session itself.

The outcomes

The distinction between the outcomes and the objectives was made clear in Chapter 4. This is (as stated above) that the outcomes of a session are the changes that happen as a result of the learning that has taken place. For example, in a session about 'job search skills' for a group of young people who are approaching school-leaving age, the *objectives* will establish what participants have the opportunity to do *during* the session, but the *outcomes* for participants *following* the session might include:

- an increase in confidence when looking for jobs;
- a broader knowledge and understanding of where and how to look for jobs;
- a decision about what action to take in relation to job search;
- an action step (e.g. sending an introductory letter and CV to a range of employers).

Law (2001) describes a model that may be applied to the analysis of personal learning and development outcomes. The model identifies a framework constituting four parts which, when linked, offer optimum opportunity for success in relation to making informed choices about our lives and taking action on the decisions we make. This framework is known as the DOTS model:

D = decision making (what can/should I do?)

O = opportunity awareness (what options are available to me?)

T = transition skills (what changes have I made and how have I coped?)

S = self-awareness (what are my issues, strengths, ideas, skills, abilities, and so on?)

When examined chronologically, the acronym changes somewhat:

1   The development of *self-awareness* is key to understanding ourselves in relation to others and in the context of our lives, hopes and concerns (S)

2   Once we are clearer about who we are, we can begin to explore the *options* that are available to us (O)

3   When we know what the options are, we can make a *decision* about what action we need to take (D)

4   Finally, we will act on the decision we have made in relation to the options that are available to us; thus, we have made a *transition* (T).

Law's (2004) thinking has moved on, but this is not to dismiss the DOTS model as outdated and of little use. Quite the reverse. The model can be used in order to evaluate the outcomes of PLD sessions. As a result of the session, for example, have the participants gained and applied greater self-awareness? Have the young people become increasingly aware of the options that are available to them and considered these in more depth? Are they able to make decisions about changes in their lives, using their heightened understanding of themselves and the options available to them? And, finally, have the participants acted on the decisions they have made? The answers to these questions may not be apparent at the end of the PLD session. For example, a *transition* will not have taken place during the group work. It is only later, as a result of the learning that has taken place in the session and following it, will young people have the opportunity to apply their learning. Similarly, *self-awareness* may have been developed during the session, but the way in which this new self-awareness is applied in a 'real-life' situation can only be assessed after the session has taken place.

If, therefore, the outcomes of the session are not realized until a point in the future, attempting an evaluation of them at the end of each PLD session is fruitless. Whereas the extent to which the objectives have been met can be analysed during and at the end of the session, the outcomes cannot be verified immediately. The youth support worker should allow time to pass in order that outcomes are achieved, before attempting to evaluate them. This can be tricky. Whereas completion of an evaluation form or exercise at the end of a PLD session is a relatively straightforward business, organizing an analysis of outcomes after time has lapsed can be somewhat problematic as young people can be difficult to 'track down' and may need prompting to complete and return forms. There are though some possible strategies that can be implemented:

- Organize a follow-up session with the participants that reflects on learning and identifies action taken as a result of the PLD group work.

- Send out questionnaires to participants asking them how their learning has had an impact in real terms.

- Meet participants individually to evaluate their learning and to offer further support should it be required.

- Ask participants to take part in introducing similar PLD group work to other young people in order to share their experiences of how the session has helped them.

- Invite feedback from colleagues who also work with the young people to assess the changes that have taken place.

By implementing one, or a combination of these strategies, a helpful insight into the outcomes achieved by the young people should be provided. Again, it is the responsibility of the youth support worker to reflect on the information they have received regarding the outcomes for the participants and to make changes and adaptations in the planning of future sessions as appropriate. One final point about the importance of evaluating outcomes should be made. Youth support workers are under increasing pressure (as are all education professionals) to *evidence* the effectiveness of their work. By providing data on the outcomes achieved in PLD group sessions (perhaps by using the DOTS model as a framework), practitioners will have a strong argument for continuing to develop this area of work in the institution. If results can be observed and verified (greater self-awareness, greater understanding of options, the ability to make informed decisions, the motivation to make changes and other outcomes that may not have been envisaged as part of the design), then the work that has been undertaken by the youth support worker will be valued and can be developed so that other young people can also gain from the experience.

The structure and activities

In addition to evaluating how far the session objectives have been met and assessing the positive outcomes of the PLD session, the youth support worker should also reflect on the detail of the session itself. In particular, the structure of the session and the activities that were planned should be examined to ensure that optimum learning took place. It is only by putting the session 'under the microscope' that youth support workers can undertake a critical analysis of their work and decide how effectively it meets the needs of the participants.

A useful starting point for evaluating the session itself is to focus on the structure. By reflecting back on the session plan, which should have identified the content and timings of each of the three stages of the group work (see Chapter 6), the youth support worker will have the opportunity to consider the following:

- How effectively did the session 'hang together' or flow?
- How realistic were the timings?
- How clear were participants about the session focus at the end of stage one?
- To what extent did participants have the opportunity to reflect on their own position in relation to the topic in stage two?
- Was there enough time allocated for planning action in stage three?

Depending on the answers to these questions, development and adjustment of the session can take place. Youth support workers who deliver PLD sessions often find that the two stages requiring further work are stages one and three. This may be because it takes longer to establish the purpose of the session and the ground rules in stage one than expected and therefore stage three can become rushed or 'squeezed'. It is important to try to remain objective when evaluating the minutiae of the session. In the immediate aftermath, it may feel as though the session was chaotic and unfocused. However, it is likely that even when this is the case, minor adjustments to the structure will improve the session significantly. If planning and preparation has been rigorous in the first place, then 'tweaking' of timings or activities should be enough to ensure that the session is fit for purpose. Youth support workers should avoid the urge to tear up the session plan and start all over again!

Linked to the evaluation of the structure of the session is the need to establish how effectively the activities and methods of delivery met the needs of the participants, enabling personal learning and development to take place. In particular, the youth support worker will want to know:

- How effectively did the activities engage the participants?
- How appropriate were the activities for the range of ability levels in the group?
- Were there activities that were not effective? Why?
- Were there activities that should have been developed? Why? How?
- How much did the activities contribute to the personal learning and development of the participants?

It is helpful to build up a 'bank' of activities that work well, which can be adapted and transposed to a range of topics. Similarly, if an activity has failed to engage the participants and has contributed nothing to the session, serious thought should be given to how it is used in the future.

Having evaluated the extent to which the objectives have been met, the outcomes for participants and the detail of the session, there is one element remaining that should be critically analysed; the performance and skills of the facilitator.

The facilitator's performance

Clearly, the approach, style, skills and techniques adopted by the facilitator will have a significant impact on the success of the session. Geldard and Geldard assert that:

> Evaluation of leadership styles and models of practice provides the most effective means for leaders to discover ways to develop their skills, modify their leadership behaviours and amend their management of group processes.
>
> (Geldard and Geldard, 2001: 148)

It can be difficult to turn a magnifying glass on ourselves and to be honest and open about what we did well and what could be improved in our group sessions. Facilitators may be tempted to take rather limiting approaches to this aspect of the evaluation process. Common unhelpful responses to reflection on personal performance might include:

- I was rubbish! I did not handle that well at all.
- The group was rubbish! It was impossible to work with those young people.
- If only the room/the facilities/the equipment (delete as necessary) had been better, I would have been fine.
- I never wanted to work with groups in the first place. I knew that it would all go wrong.
- That was great. I had a ball. Next!

Nelson-Jones suggests that:

> Some leaders may be so intent on validating their efforts that they selectively perceive positive feedback and give it too much weight. At the other extreme are leaders who discount successes and dwell excessively on shortcomings.
>
> (Nelson-Jones, 1991: 282)

In fact, what is required is a systematic analysis of the interaction between the group and the facilitator. Useful questions for reflection might include:

1   How well did I engage with the group?
2   How effectively did I gain and maintain the participants' attention?
3   How clearly did I introduce the session?

4 How effectively did I negotiate the contract/ground rules?

5 How clearly did I explain activities? Did the participants know what they had to do and why they were doing it?

6 How effectively did I enable personal learning by facilitating activities?

7 How well did I manage conflict in the group?

8 How well did I respond to *all* group members, not just the vocal minority?

9 Were there times in the session when my anxiety levels were raised? How did I manage?

10 On a scale of 1–10 (1 being terrible, 10 being fantastic), how would I rate my performance? What could I do to score higher?

In each case the supplementary question 'what could I have done differently?' should also be considered. However experienced and confident youth support workers are in their group work skills, there is always room for improvement and development. Where those who are new to the role are likely to overanalyse and be critical of their skills, those who have facilitated numerous group sessions may be more likely to keep evaluation brief or 'skip it' altogether. Both approaches are unhelpful and limiting. Of course, evaluation takes time and, as youth support workers will know, time is often in very short supply. However, investing in a thorough evaluation at this stage will pay dividends in the future when the answer to the 'what could I have done differently?' question is implemented.

It is important at this stage to move on to consider not only *what* should be evaluated and *why*, but also *how* the evaluation might take place.

Evaluation methods and techniques

There are a range of methods, techniques and activities that youth support workers can use both in the session and following it to gain feedback from participants about how effective the session has been. Some of these methods can be implemented as part of the session itself (in order to evaluate the session objectives, the content and the facilitator's skills and approach), and others can be used following the session (in order to evaluate the personal learning and development outcomes).

As part of the planning, youth support workers should include activities to elicit feedback on the content of the session and the learning taking place. There are numerous ways that this feedback can be extracted. For example, most facilitators are likely, at some point, to use participant evaluation questionnaires at the end of the session. These are useful, but there are other creative ways to encourage participants to share their ideas about the session. Table 10.1 shows a number of different evaluation methods and techniques that could be used both during and after the session.

There may already be recommended evaluation documentation (evaluation forms or questionnaires) that the institution prefers those who undertake group sessions to use. Experienced colleagues can also be a useful source of ideas for interesting and varied methods of evaluating the effectiveness of PLD group work. It is

Table 10.1 Methods of evaluation

Evaluation during the session	Evaluation following the session
• Where the session is part of a programme of PLD group work, suggest that participants keep a reflective diary/log of their learning that can be summarized and shared at the end • Complete individual participant evaluation forms • Undertake an evaluation activity in pairs or small groups and present it back on flip-charts • Use symbols rather than words to encourage evaluation. For example, four large sheets of paper are hung around the room. One has a smiley face, one a frowning face, one an expressionless face and one a light bulb. Invite participants to make comments on the sheet that most closely reflects how the participant feels about the session (with any ideas for development on the light bulb sheet) • Use 'sticky' notes for participants to write up comments and stick them on the walls for others to read • Whole group discussion about the session objectives and how far they have been met • Include an activity whereby participants make focused comments about the session and what they have learned via a 'video diary', which can be shared with other young people or staff	• Conduct individual interviews with participants following the session • Send out questionnaires to participants one month after the session has taken place • Reconvene the group one month after the session has taken place to evaluate the outcomes • Involve significant others in the evaluation – teachers, other youth support workers, heads of year, parents/carers, by meeting to discuss their perceptions of the impact of the PLD session • Complete a facilitator's self-evaluation questionnaire • Refer back to the reflective diary/log that you have kept

important to be aware that attention should be paid to the literacy levels and learning needs within the group. Wordy evaluation forms, for example, may not be appropriate for young people who require support with language. Included here are some examples of evaluation forms and questionnaires that can be used to elicit feedback and evaluate PLD group sessions. They offer a starting point for those who are not familiar with the process of evaluation or are looking for new approaches.

Example 1

EVALUATION FORM: Please complete the form as fully as you can so that the session can be developed further and additional support can be provided

---

SESSION OBJECTIVES:

NAME:

How helpful was the session to you at this point in time?
Name three things that you learned from the session:
How will what you have learned help you in the future?
What did you enjoy about the session?
What else would you have liked to have done in the session?
What would you leave out or change about the session?
What further sessions would be helpful?

Example 1 is a broad-ranging evaluation tool which, when completed fully, will provide the youth support worker with valuable information not only about the session itself, but also about any future support needs that participants might have. In addition, it will encourage the young person to reflect on their learning.

The statements in Example 2 enable reflection and the scoring is simple and easy for young people to use. The statements are written in a positive way to encourage young people to focus their thinking on what they achieved in the session. However, although the box at the end of the form makes space for 'additional comments', young people may choose not to explain the scores they have awarded. This can be

---

Example 2

EVALUATION FORM: Please circle the appropriate response to each statement where
1 = strongly agree, 2 = agree, 3 = unsure, 4 = disagree, 5 = strongly disagree

Session title:

Name:

Scoring	Strongly agree = 1	Agree = 2	Unsure = 3	Disagree = 4	Strongly disagree = 5
The session was helpful	1	2	3	4	5
I have learned things that will make a difference to me	1	2	3	4	5
The session was interesting	1	2	3	4	5
The session was fun	1	2	3	4	5
The facilitator helped me to get involved	1	2	3	4	5
Overall I would rate this session as being enjoyable and helpful	1	2	3	4	5

Additional comments:

frustrating, particularly if participants have awarded scores of 4 or 5 against specific statements. Because of the quantitative format (i.e. scores being used for each statement so that the levels of response are quantified), youth support workers could undertake an overall group evaluation by using the statistical information that the forms provide.

Example 3

EVALUATION FORM: Please respond as fully as you can to the questions below. I will send you a copy of this form that you can keep as a reminder of the action you have agreed to take

Session title:

Session objectives:

Name:

What did you learn in the session?

What action do you need to take as a result of the session:

- tomorrow?
- in the next week?
- in the next month?

What help and support will you need?

Who will you go to for this help and support?
How will you know that your actions have been successful?

This evaluation tool in Example 3 fulfils a range of functions. Not only does it encourage the young people to reflect on their learning, but it also provides a framework for them to plan action steps for the future. In addition, it helps the youth support worker to evaluate the session and to consider how the young person will need to be supported in the future. However, it focuses less on what actually happened in the session to enable learning to take place.

FACILITATOR'S SELF-EVALUATION
Session title:
Session objectives:
How accurate was the assessment of needs and how relevant was the topic?

How well was the session structured? Any changes in the future?
Which activities worked well and which require development?
How far were the session objectives met?
What skills did I use and which could I have used more?
How did I manage challenging behaviour and the group dynamic?
What further action/support do I need to take as a result of this session?

By using a form such as this as a starting point for self-evaluation, the facilitator's reflections can be focused and in depth.

Although quite different in emphasis and tone, these sample forms each have value. My own view is that qualitative data (i.e. responses to open questions) is rich and helpful, both in encouraging the young people to reflect on their learning during the session and enabling youth support workers to develop their practice. The quantitative methods, although quick and easy to complete, provide less in the way of suggestions for development.

Summary

So, although the PLD session is over, the young people have collected their belongings and the room is empty, the facilitator's work is not yet complete. The youth support worker should set time aside to reflect on the session that has taken place, using the responses of the participants that have been shared in an evaluation activity/questionnaire as a starting point. This should not be viewed simply as a 'paper' exercise whereby the youth support worker can provide data on the session should it be required. Rather, evaluation should be valued as an integral part of the learning process, feeding into the development of future sessions and the ongoing support of young people. Time spent in evaluation is time well spent. Future sessions are likely to be even more enjoyable, and importantly, more successful as a result.

This book has sought to act as a guide to youth support workers in planning, preparing and delivering their PLD sessions with young people. But there is only so much that a resource like this can offer. No amount of advice and guidance can replicate the actual experience of 'doing' group work. However, at the very least, those who undertake group work should feel confident that they have done everything in their power to ensure that the experience is a positive and enjoyable one for the young people – and for themselves!

> **Activity**
>
> Use the self-evaluation proforma in this chapter as a tool for reflection on the last PLD session you undertook.

References

Adams, J. (1993) Group work in the youth service, in K. Dwivedi (ed.) *Group Work with Children and Adolescents*. London: Jessica Kingsley.

Ali, S. (2003) *Mixed-race, Post-race, Gender, New Ethnicities and Cultural Practice*. London: Berg.

Amundson, N., Harris-Bowlesby, J. and Niles, S. (2008) *Essential Elements of Career Counselling: Processes and Technique*. Englewood Cliffs, NJ: Prentice Hall.

Arnold, C. and Yeomans, J. (2004) *Psychology for Teaching Assistants*. Stoke-on-Trent: Trentham Books.

Barlow, C., Blyth, J. and Edmonds, M. (1998) *A Handbook of Interactive Exercises for Groups*. Boston, MA: Allyn & Bacon.

Bee, H. and Boyd, D. (2002) *Lifespan Development*. Boston: Allyn & Bacon.

Belbin, R.M. (1993) *Team Roles at Work*. Oxford: Butterworth Heinemann.

Bentley, T. (1994) *Facilitation: Providing Opportunities For Learning*. London: McGraw-Hill.

Bion, W.R. (1961) *Experiences in Groups*. London: Tavistock/Routledge.

Blatchford, P. (1998) *Social Life in School: Pupils Experiences from 7 to 16 Years*. London: Falmer Press.

Bolton, G. (2005) *Reflective Practice: Writing and Professional Development*, 2nd edn. London: Sage Publications.

Boud, D., Keogh, R. and Walker, D. (1985) *Reflection: Turning Experience into Learning*. London: Kogan Page.

Bradbury, A. (2006) *Successful Presentation Skills*, 3rd edn. London: Kogan Page.

Brandes, D. and Ginnis, P. (1996) *A Guide to Student-centred Learning*. Cheltenham: Nelson Thornes.

Brandes, D. and Norris, J. (1998) *The Gamester's Handbook 3*. Cheltenham: Nelson Thornes.

Brookfield, S. (2006) *The Skillful Teacher*. San Francisco, LA: Jossey-Bass.

Brown, R. (1995) *Prejudice: Its Social Psychology*. Oxford: Blackwell.

Bruegel, I. (2005) Diversity as a constraint on social capital formation: a study of english schoolchildren. Conference paper, CRONEM: The Future of Multicultural Britain, June.

Clifford, S. and Herrmann, A. (1999) *Making a Leap: Theatre of Empowerment*. London: Jessica Kingsley.

Coffield, F., Mosely, D., Hall, E. and Ecclestone, K. (2004) *Learning Styles and Pedagogy in Post-16 Learning: A Systematic and Critical Review*. London: Learning and Skills Research Centre.

Coleman, J.C. and Hendry, L.B. (1999) *The Nature of Adolescence*, 3rd edn. London: Routledge.

Davies, B. (2005) Youth work: a manifesto for our time, *Youth and Policy*, 88: 5–27. Leicester: The National Youth Agency.

de Shazer, S. (1994) *Words were Originally Magic*. New York: W.W. Norton.

Department for Education and Skills (2003) *Citizenship: The National Curriculum for England*. London: DfES.

Dewey, J. (1938) *Experience and Education*. New York: Collier Books.

Doel, M. (2006) *Using Groupwork*. London: Routledge.

Draley, S. and Heath, W. (2007) *The Expressive Arts Activity Book: A Resource for Professionals*. London: Jessica Kingsley.

Dunn, R. (2005) *Dos and Don'ts of Behaviour Management*. London: Continuum International Publishing Group.

Egan, G. (1973) *Face to Face: The Small-group Experience and Interpersonal Growth*. California: Brooks/Cole.

Egan, G. (2002) *The Skilled Helper: A Problem-management and Opportunity-development Approach to Helping*, 7th edn. Pacific Grove, CA: Brooks/Cole.

Entwistle, N. (1988) *Styles of Learning and Teaching*. London: David Fulton.

Fatout, M.F. (1996) *Children in Groups: A Social Work Perspective*. Connecticut: Auburn House.

Freud, S. (1921) *Group Psychology and the Analysis of the Ego*. New York: Bantam Press.

Fuchs, B. (2002) *Group Games: Social Skills*. Bicester: Speechmark.

Gardner, H. (1993), *Frames of Mind*, 2nd edn. New York: Basic Books.

Geldard, K. and Geldard, D. (2001) *Working with Children in Groups*. Basingstoke: Palgrave.

Gerrity, D.A. and DeLucia-Waack, J.L. (2007) Effectiveness of groups in the schools, *The Journal for Specialists in Group Work*, 32 (1): 97–106.

Hadfield, J. (1992) *Classroom Dynamics*. Oxford: Oxford University Press.

Harper, P. (1993) Developmental considerations in therapeutic provisions, in K. Dwivedi (ed.) *Group Work with Children and Adolescents*. London: Jessica Kingsley.

Hermann, N. (1996) *The Whole Brain Business Book*. New York: McGraw-Hill.

Higgins, R. and Westergaard, J. (2001) The role of group work in careers education and guidance programmes, *Career Research and Development*, 2: 4–17. Cambridge: CRAC.

Honey, P. and Mumford, A. (2000) *The Learning Styles Helper's Guide*. Maidenhead: Peter Honey Publications Ltd.

Jeffs, T. (2004) Curriculum debate: a letter to John Ord., *Youth and Policy*, 84: 55–61. Leicester: The National Youth Agency.

Jennings, S. (1986) *Creative Drama in Groupwork*. Bicester: Winslow Press.

Johnson, D.W. and Johnson, F.P. (1997) *Joining Together: Group Theory and Group Skills*, 6th edn. Boston, MA: Allyn & Bacon.

Kehily, M.J. (2007) *Understanding Youth: Perspectives, Identities and Practice*. London: Sage Publications.

Killick, S. (2006) *Emotional Literacy at the Heart of the School Ethos*. London: Paul Chapman Publishing.

Kolb, D.A. (1984) *Experiential Learning: Experience as the Source of Learning and Development*. Englewood Cliffs, NJ: Prentice Hall.

Kurland, R. (2002) Racial difference and human commonality: the worker–client relationship, *Social Work with Groups*, 25(1/2): 113–18.

Law, B. (2001) *New thinking for Connexions and Citizenship*. Cambridge: The Career Learning Network.

Law, B. (2004) Careers education and citizenship: for tinker, taylor, worker and citizen, *Careers*

Education and Citizenship: An Inclusive Agenda. Canterbury Christ Church University Occasional Paper: 27–34.

Lewin, K. (1951) *Resolving Social Conflicts.* USA: American Psychological Association.

Lewin, K., Lippitt, R. and White, R.K. (1994) Patterns or aggressive behaviour in experimentally created 'social climates', *Journal of Social Psychology,* 10: 217–99.

Liebmann, M. (2008) *Art Therapy for Groups: A Handbook of Themes and Exercises,* 2nd edn. Hove: Brunner-Routledge.

Lowery, N.V. (2003) Reflective teaching, *New Teacher Advocate,* 11(2): 8.

Malekoff, A. (2004) *Group Work with Children and Adolescents: Principles and Practice.* New York: Guilford Press.

Mennuti, R., Freeman, A and Christner, R.W. (2006) *Cognitive-behavioural Interventions in Educational Settings.* Oxon: Routledge.

Miller, N. and Boud, D. (1996) *Working with Experience.* London: Routledge.

Myers, I.B. and McCaulley, M.H. (1998) *Manual: A Guide to the Development and Use of the Myers-Briggs Type Indicator.* Palo Alto, CA: Consulting Psychologists Press.

Nelson-Jones, R. (1991) *Lifeskills: A Handbook.* London: Cassell.

Nelson-Jones, R. (2005) *Theory and Practice of Counselling and Therapy,* 4th edn. London: Sage Publications.

Payne, M. (2005) Working with groups, in R. Harrison and C. Wise (eds.) *Working with Young People.* London: Sage Publications.

Piaget, J. (1971) *Child's Conception of the World.* London: Paladin.

Plummer, D.M. (2007) *Self-esteem Games for Children.* London: Jessica Kingsley.

Pritchard, A. (2005) *Ways of Learning.* London: David Fulton.

Redl, F. (1972) *When We Deal with Children: Selected Writings.* New York: The Free Press.

Reid, H.L. (2005) Narrative and career guidance: beyond small talk and towards useful dialogue for the 21st century, *International Journal for Vocational and Educational Guidance,* 5: 125–36.

Reid, H.L. and Fielding, A.J. (2007) *Providing Support to Young People: A Guide to Interviewing in Helping Relationships.* London: Sage Publications.

Reynolds, M. (1994) *Groupwork in Education and Training.* London: Kogan Page.

Rogers, B. (1998) *You Know the Fair Rule,* 2nd edn. London: Financial Times, Prentice Hall.

Rogers, C. (1965) *Client-centred Therapy.* Boston, MA: Houghton Mifflin.

Schon, D.A. (1990) *The Reflective Practitioner: How Professionals Think in Action.* San Francisco, LA: Jossey-Bass.

Scruton, R. (1987) Expressionist education, *Oxford Review of Education,* 13(1): 39–44.

Slavin, R.L. (1997) A group analysis approach to the education of children and teenagers, *Journal of Child and Adolescence Group Therapy,* 7(2): 69–78.

Smith, A. (1996) *Accelerated Learning in the Classroom.* Stafford: Network Educational Press Ltd.

Sue, D.W. and Sue, D. (1999) *Counselling the Culturally Different: Theory and Practice,* 3rd edn. New York: Wiley.

Tew, M., Read, M. and Potter, H. (2007) *Circles, PHSE and Citizenship: Assessing the Value of Circle Time in Secondary Schools.* London: Paul Chapman Publishing.

Tuckman, B.W. (1965) Developmental sequence in small groups, *Psychological Bulletin,* 63: 384–99.

Tuckman, B.W. and Jensen, M.A.C. (1977) Stages in small group development, *Group and Organisational Studies,* 2: 419–27.

Vermunt, J.D. (1994) *Inventory of Learning Styles (ILS) in Higher Education.* Tilburg: University of Tilburg.

Vernelle, B. (1994) *Understanding and Using Groups.* London: Whiting & Birch.

Westergaard, J. (2005) Counselling and the youth support worker role – are these connected? in R. Harrison and C. Wise (eds) *Working with Young People*. London: Sage Publications.

Westergaard, J. (2007) Guidance through group work: delivering personalised learning and development in the group context. Conference paper, IAEVG: Padua, September.

Williamson, H. (2005) Challenging practice: a personal view on 'youth work' in times of changed expectations, in R. Harrison and C. Wise (eds) *Working with Young People*. London: Sage Publications.

Winslade, J. and Monk, G. (2000) *Narrative Mediation*. San Francisco, LA: Jossey-Bass.

Young, J. (2005) *100 Ideas for Managing Behaviour*. London: Continuum International Publishing Group.

Index

IMPROVING BEHAVIOUR AND ATTENDANCE AT SCHOOL

Susan Hallam and Lynne Rogers

Behaviour remains a huge issue of concern at all levels of education. This book draws together research and practice to uncover the complexities of improving behaviour and attendance in school and offers a range of practical solutions aimed at tackling behavioural issues and its prevention for schools, teachers, non-teaching staff, and those working to support them in Local Authorities.

It considers current concerns relating to the behaviour of children and young people, the theoretical underpinnings of possible approaches to improving behaviour and attendance, as well as what we know about the causes of disaffection. In exploring ways that behaviour and attendance can be improved, the authors examine a range of perspectives including school management and whole school policies, and behaviour in and around the school, in the classroom, and of individual pupils, particularly those at risk of exclusion from school.

It discusses the work of Behaviour and Educational Support Teams, teacher coaches, learning mentors and nurture groups as ways of supporting children and young people, particularly those identified as being 'at risk'. It also outlines ways of improving relationships between the school and home, as well as the ways that parents can be supported to assist in changing their children's behaviour and attendance. Alternatives to exclusion and new curricula are discussed in relation to their success in maintaining students in education.

The final chapters focus on attendance and what can be done to improve it in the general school population and those students who are persistent absentees. Throughout the book case studies are used to illustrate examples of good practice and the impact on children, parents and teachers. The book concludes with an overview of key issues emerging for practice.

Contents
Section 1: The context – Background – Theoretical underpinnings and the causes of poor behaviour – Section 2: Improving behaviour – Management and whole school policies – Behaviour in and around school – Home-school relationships – Supporting parents through the use of parenting programmes – Behaviour in the classroom – Alternative curricula – Supporting at risk children – Approaches to exclusion – Section 3: Improving attendance – Whole school approaches to attendance – Working with persistent absentees – Section 4: Overview – Overview.

2008   312pp
978-0-335-22242-1 (Paperback)   978-0-335-22241-4 (Hardback)

LADS AND LADETTES IN SCHOOL

Carolyn Jackson

This innovative book looks at how and why girls and boys adopt 'laddish' behaviours in schools. It examines the ways in which students negotiate pressures to be popular and 'cool' in school alongside pressures to perform academically. It also deals with the fears of academic and social failure that influence pupils' school lives and experiences.

Drawing extensively on the voices of students in secondary schools, it explores key questions about laddish behaviours, such as:

- Are girls becoming more laddish – and if so, which girls?
- Do boys and girls have distinctive versions of laddishness?
- Do laddish behaviours lead to the same outcomes?
- What are the implications for teachers and schools?

The author weaves together key contemporary theories and research on masculinities and femininities with social and psychological theories and research on academic motives and goals, in order to understand the complexities of girls' and boys' behaviours.

This topical book is key reading for students, academics and researchers in education, sociology and psychology, as well as school teachers and education policy makers.

Contents

Introduction – Part 1: Theoretical frameworks: motives and behaviours – Academic motives: achievement goal theory and self-worth protection – Social motives: constructing 'appropriate' masculinities and femininities – The interplay between academic and gender identities – Part 2: From theory to practice and back again – Testing times: pressures and fears at school – School work or 'cool' work: competing goals at school – Self-defence: techniques and strategies for protecting self-worth – Balancing acts: who can balance the books and a social life? – Part 3: Implications and ways forward – Implications for teachers today – Implications for the policy makers of tomorrow – Conclusions

176pp   0 335 21770 2 (Paperback)   0 335 21771 0 (Hardback)

NEW PERSPECTIVES ON BULLYING

Helen Cowie and Dawn Jennifer

- What is bullying?
- What can we learn from research findings?
- What are the risk factors for bullying or being bullied?
- How can we take account of the voice of the child?
- How can educators, policy-makers, health professionals and parents work together with children and young people to prevent and reduce bullying?

This book provides a valuable resource for anyone responsible for the emotional health and well-being of children and young people. The authors focus on the importance of fostering positive relationships in the school community as a whole, so that young people and adults feel empowered to challenge bullying when they encounter it and protect those involved.

Using case studies of real experiences, innovative practice, key research findings and perspectives from children and young people themselves, the authors provide perceptive insights into the positive ways of relating to others that are essential if we are to address the issue of bullying successfully. The material outlined in the book is directly linked to the new agenda for change in meeting the needs of the child, empowering children to be consulted and to take responsibility for issues that affect them. It explores a range of effective interventions that can counteract bullying – including restorative approaches; peer mediation; narrative approaches; and cyber support.

Key features include:

- Chapter overviews
- Examples of effective practice
- Summaries of key research findings
- Children's views and experiences
- Learning points at the end of each chapter
- List of related organisations, websites and resources to support interventions against bullying

Practical guidance based on sound evaluation is provided - as well as an insight into international perspectives on bullying - to help develop a positive school environment and disseminate good practice.

New Perspectives on Bullying is an indispensable resource for teachers, researchers, health professionals, social workers and parents.

Contents
Acknowledgements – Knowledge about school bullying – The whole-school approach – Working with the relationship to help the bullied pupil – Working with the relationship to change bullying behaviour – Working with the relationship to help the whole class – Peers helping peers – The role of narrative – Creating a supportive environment – References – Subject index – Name index.

2008   176pp
978-0-335-22244-5 (Paperback)   978-0-335-22243-8 (Hardback)